Heinrich Eliyahu Benedikt

Spirituality versus Religion

Principles of Interreligious Understanding and Self-Realization

Lotus Publications

Heinrich Eliyahu Benedikt

Spirituality versus Religion

Principles of Interreligious Understanding and Self-Realization

Lotus Publications

First Edition 1995

Typeset: CSF · ComputerSatz GmbH, Freiburg im Breisgau
Printing and Binding: freiburger graphische betriebe, Freiburg im Breisgau
Printed in Germany
ISBN 3-931470-00-8

Preface

Dear and esteemed Reader,

This short manuscript was written within three weeks at the end of the summer of 1995. It came into being as a response to conversations that the author had with several scholars and religious authorities of different traditions. It also was meant to be a response to one of the major problems of our days.

In this age of quickly growing social, economic, psychological and ethical instability and decay, paralleled with a worldwide-felt lack of meaning and orientation in one's own life, we can observe an increasing quest or search for identity. Behind the background of this worldwide uncertainty many repressed questions arise: Where is this world and society of ours heading? Where will the course of destiny and life bring us? What is the purpose and meaning of our human life? Who am I? Where do I come from? Where am I going?

Such questions naturally lead us to a return and rediscovery of the ancient sources of our religious traditions. In the perennial inheritance of their teachings, divine wisdom and revelation, we ought to find a source of light, inspiration and guidance which illuminates our quest and reveals the deeper meaning of our temporary journey through this world. Unfortunately, this search and return to our religious tradition, if it does not go hand-in-hand with an introspective manner or honest and sincere questioning, reconsideration and change of our own expectations, inner values and attitudes towards ourselves, God, life and our fellow man, remains very superficial. Instead of inducing an overall renewal of our outlook towards life, meaning, vocation and eternity, towards our relationship with God, self and our fellow man, it very often leads to religious fanaticism and fundamentalism based on the unreflected adaptation of religious dogmas generated by the unchanged patterns of the cold and intolerant worldly attitudes and egotism dominating our ignorant minds.

Rising nationalism and religious fundamentalism are the main responses of these hidden patterns of our collective unconscious to the identity crisis of our times. If I speak about fundamentalism, I do not confine this term, like many Western commentators do, to Islam but also apply it to frozen orthodox Judaism and Christianity (including the modern movement of "second-born" people), as well as to radical Hindus. Watching these developments with alert awareness, we face the degeneration of religions to mere ideological powers and the religious institutions to political party-like lobbies, fostering specific interests of partial groups rather than serving to guide and enlighten mankind.

Instead of striving for an inner change and realization, a revolution in their own minds and souls, many people force different theological opinions and dogmas on others. Instead of turning inside, they turn even more excessivly outside, missionizing and superimposing their "new ideology" upon their victims. Instead of becoming a pole of peace or a pillar of light and a man or woman of love and compassion, they even project their own impurities and iniquities onto the world, thus increasing its misery and becoming tormentors to those who differ in creed and belief.

In this way religious groups still ignore and often fight each other, claiming to be in sole possession of truth, divine revelation and the key for redemption. Most of the wars in our world today are motivated by religious beliefs, especially in Israel, Yugoslavia and India. There such religious claims have become the major obstacles to peace and coexistence between people of different creeds. Following the collapse of communist totalitarianism in several parts of the world, the growing nationalistic and fundamentalistic movements of our planet are on the march to becoming a serious threat to world peace and personal freedom.

The need and calling of our times is for a clear step from dogmatic religion to spiritual awareness, from outward-oriented intellectual behaviorism and projecting minds to an inwardly-turned consciousness. It is not "shoulds" and "have to's," blind beliefs and mental concepts about God, life and self that can bring us joy, peace and understanding, but clear perception, inner experience and a taste of God which can bring about a true and valid change in our lives. Without honest self-examination and deep meditation one cannot discriminate and realize "Truth." And without a shift from mere "beliefs" and "mental concepts" to a deep soul-awareness, from abstract theological speculations to a profound inner experience of the Divine, light will not penetrate into our darkness.

We need to spiritualize our lives, to strive for a wakeful awareness which watches over all the movements within the kingdom of our soul and to charge our lives with cosmic love and divine light. This is spirituality: to turn within, in order to discover the eternal source of all love and light, to develop virtues of purity and to express and radiate this love and light and these virtues in our thoughts, words and actions. An attitude of universality, service and all-embracing love is the unspoken proof of a truly spiritual life. Only such an inner transformation and realization can bring about peace and understanding and can ultimately lead to a solution of the uncountable problems of our world today. In this way we may fulfill the purpose of our life to attain wisdom, peace and happiness. This is the challenge of our time: to overcome religious dogmatism by direct experience of God and, through that, to make a definite shift to an entirely spiritual-oriented life. Without this shift, religious statements and ceremonies are only sugarcoating on our unchanged bestial nature. Without this shift to a real inner change, mankind will not survive the increasing problems of the coming age. It is my hope that with God's help this little booklet may be able to draw some light onto this subject.

Table of Contents

I.

Some Basic Preliminaries for the Path of Divine Life, Meditation and Self-Realization

Religious behavior must not be allowed to compromise our natural moral sensitivities. If indeed it does, then it is clearly misguided. We know that our behavior is derived from pure and spiritual motives when our innate sense of what is right becomes the more exalted as a consequence of its religious inspiration. If the opposite occurs and the moral quality of the individual and public response is diminished by our religious observance, then we are certainly mistaken in our path and our supposed piety is of no value.

Rav Abraham Kook

For many, many centuries thousands of seeking souls of every creed and culture all over the world have spent many years or even whole lifetimes reading, studying, interpreting and discussing the sacred scriptures of their specific religion and arguing about religious matters and eternal questions of life and existence. Over the ages many scholars have written philosophical tracts and scientific treatises about religion and God that have laid the foundations for their own wealth and fame, but not helped them to realize or touch the one ultimate reality, the One Living God, who is the creator of all beings and the only true source of all religions. And if someone came and questioned their knowledge or reputation, many of them lost their dispassion and went into a fit of temper, proving to have an ordinary mind filled with pride and worldly desires rather than a state of God-realization.

True religion, in the spiritual sense, is like the philosopher's stone which transforms and changes the souls and the minds, with all of their faculties, of those who come in touch with it. This change, which in essence consists of a deep, deep inner transformation, results in a total reformation of one's understanding, feeling, thinking and, last but not least, one's attitudes towards life, all fellow men and other creatures without discriminating according to color, nation, sex, language or creed.

The task of true religion is very practical and not at all superficial; it goes straight to the very root of our being and existence. In order to bring about a real change or transformation in our lives and, therefore, also to the state of our human-made world, we have to go deeply within ourselves to the very core of our existence which is the living God. In order to succeed in this task, we have to use our sharpened perception; by using it as a tool of self-discovery we need to dive deeply into the unknown space of ourselves, penetrating all the layers of our personality and removing all the inner obstacles we find there. Having done this, we will, at last, realize the sparkling light of our true and eternal Self which, rising within our awareness, starts to flood our entire being with bliss, love, divine life, peace, humility and all of the timeless blessings that God bestows onto His true devotees. Only there, in the core of our eternal Self, far beyond our senses or mind, beyond our intellect and our will, beyond our egoistic personality, deep in the heart of our hearts can we touch or even realize the One Living God as the ultimate, only and all-pervading reality which is the source, cause, root, essence and destination of all created universes and beings.

True seekers and devotees of God are as rare as diamonds on the seashore. They are very, very rare, but sparkle with the lights of purity, humility, compassion, wisdom and selfless love. In the *Bhagavad Gita*, one of the most holy books of the Hindus, God says to Arjuna, His disciple: "Oh Arjuna, know this: of thousands of souls, there might be one who really aspires to find Me, and of thousands of real aspirants there might be only one who really knows Me."

Knowledge of God includes self-knowledge, illumination, humble character and a selfless and loving attitude toward one's fellow men and environment. A true religious life and its practice is recognized by its fruit. A man without self-awareness and self-understanding stays ignorant and blind no matter how many holy books he has read or studied, or how many deep discussions he has had with scholars, rabbis, theologians, saints or sages. God cannot be attained by mere book study or heartless recitation of prayers; He can only be found and grasped with and through the innermost virtuous essence of our being which, in most of us, is lying dormant at the very bottom of our hearts. Without true and deep-felt longing, love or devotion, without shedding thousands of tears of painful aspiration one cannot find or meet the eternal beloved of our soul. It is as King David confesses in one of his Psalms: "I am worn out with groaning, every night I drench my pillow and soak my bed with tears; my eye is wasted with grief.... The Lord has heard the sound of my weeping; he has heard my petition and will accept my prayer." (Ps. 6)

All of this is true for everyone of us, no matter whether we are male or female, poor or rich, black or white, Hindu, Jewish, Christian, Muslim or Buddhist, German, British, Russian, Arab or Chinese. Even if God created us with many different gifts, abilities and vocations and every nation and people with a specific genius or vocation, the core and essence of all of us is One. He, the One Living God, is the One and unchangeable essence of all of us. He is the Soul of our soul, the Light of our light, the I of our I and the wakeful Awareness within our dim consciousness.

Religions teach us indiscriminate love and compassion. Even if we are treated unjustly or cruelly, we are taught we should not judge or condemn our enemies and persecutors. God spoke to Moses and said, "Mine is the revenge." Rejection, discrimination or judgmentalism have never been taken as signs or attitudes of wise or enlightened beings; nor has a lack of understanding or a lack of heartfelt care and attention towards the needs, concerns and feelings of our fellow men ever been taken as a sign of true devotees of God. Knowing better than others or judging and criticizing others will never be assumed to be divine virtues, attitudes or spiritual values.

The greatest percentage of followers of most of the world's religions claim their religion to be the only true one. They think very highly of themselves and lowly about others, treating the members and fellow believers of their religion with great sympathy but ignoring or even rejecting or condemning their neighbors and fellow men who belong to a different group or religion. Men have even fought thousands of selfish and cruel wars, or executed many incredible inquisitions, trials and persecutions in the name of God and have not even been ashamed to execute total genocides in His Name. What an ignorant blasphemy – killing in the Name of God!

Approaching religion with mere mind and intellect creates seeds of many dangers. As everyone knows, mind and intellect are blind towards the sensitive matters and questions of life and love and, beyond that, towards the transcendental reality of God. Our minds can neither grasp the infinite nature of God nor the secrets of love, life or our feelings. Neither mind nor intellect can touch the transcendental and omnipresent being of God. Both of them are cold and even very cruel in their analysis, judgments and conclusions, failing to produce any awareness of the consequences and side effects of their actions and reactions. The mind and intellect of man need always to be guided by love and conscious awareness. A Chassidic saying states, "A man is not what he knows, but how deep he feels." This is very true, especially concerning matters of eternity, life and soul.

Realizing the call of a specific religion demands our readiness to transcend mind, word, intellect and understanding. Paul of Tarsus states, "The mere word kills, only the spirit makes alive." Theological study without psychological self–awareness, heart-rendered striving for God, deep prayer, meditation and inner communion will only render us as proud intellectuals who lack the rich gifts and experiences of an inner spiritual life. Neither study nor books lead us to God-realization. Only through surrendering our "self" to the living God and making ourselves into vessels of His eternal and all-pervading peace, love and compassion and living embodiments of His infinite divine virtues leads us to God-realization. God created man in order to reveal His hidden, pure spiritual glory within time and space. His inborn image, lying dormant at the bottom of our souls, should become alive and unfold within us. He, Who is perfect Being, Consciousness, Purity and Bliss, shall be revealed through us in all of our motives, feelings, thoughts, words, gestures, movements and actions. A man or woman of God is known by his or her voice, glance, walk and speech; he or she blesses the earth with each step of his or her foot.

Granted, the study and understanding of a holy book is fruitful, but only under the condition of a deep and wakeful soul-consciousness which is combined with the influx or inspiration of God's Holy Spirit or the guidance of an illumined master who has reached God-consciousness. We should never forget that religion and holy scriptures are only means or signposts to show us the way to our eternal destiny. God, though, is beyond them. The great and very far-reaching failure of the average religious understanding of our time has its roots in mere mental or exoteric approaches. There are very few souls who are ready to sacrifice themselves for total self-transformation by God and, of these, only a very few have gained the spiritual awareness needed for direct communion with God.

Many religions, especially the three occidental ones, have become obstacles to peace, tolerance and understanding instead of being efficient means for God-realization and the achievement of harmony, equal vision, unity and brotherly love within mankind. Although modern technology, transportation and communication networks have brought mankind closer together than ever before and have created new conditions of cooperation and coexistence, the rigid patterns of national and religious traditions have built unscaleable walls and deep clefts that separate man from man, nation from nation and religion from religion. Obviously we are still living in the age of the "Babylonian confusion of language" where no one understands the other.

Men of today, if accepting religion at all, make the tradition and the rules of their religion their God. They put the rules, rites, written laws and conventions above their God; they no longer weep, fast, pray and exercise devoted self-discovery and self-sacrifice in order to find and meet the beloved of their soul. They no longer have the burning desire and love to merge into His infinite eternity; instead they make books, beliefs and customs the masters of their lives, exercising mere self-rectification on the basis of their beliefs instead of changing their hearts, minds and attitudes. They think highly of themselves and lowly of others, instead of the opposite, and believe themselves to be saved and the others to be damned – this is nothing but pure fundamentalism! Taking a religious system or set of laws and beliefs to be higher or more important than God is idolatry.

Nowadays we find this pattern in all of the religious traditions, equally in Christianity, Judaism, Islam, etc.

The place that should be taken by the One God, His Divine Light, His Living Presence and His All-transforming Spirit is occupied by rules, rites, dogmas and tradition! Walking through the streets of Jerusalem, I often find people declaring, "God is Muslim," "God is a Zionist," "God is Catholic," "Moshe is the only true prophet," "Christ (Jesus) is the only begotten Son and Redeemer," "Mohammed is the last and eternal word and act of God," etc., etc., etc. Why do we need declarations like these? Why do we need to exclude others? Instead of seeing and evaluating people by their qualities of heart and virtues of character, we judge and reject them because of their race, creed and belief. We no longer feel and look to see what a man is in his heart, feeling or seeing whether he is in a living relationship with God and his fellow men. What a sad world.

God cannot be reduced to any "ism," religion or belief or be cut down into pieces. God is above and beyond the phenomena of outer appearance or discrimination. He is looking into the hearts of men and reading the deepest thoughts and feelings of our souls. He does not care for declarations, nor does He judge by appearance; He simply goes by our hearts. If our hearts are in God then we automatically live according to His principles; if only our minds are in Him, we are not in full accordance with His will and principles.

People pray to God thinking and hoping that He will take sides in their expectations, demands, ideas or desires. They think Allah will protect the Muslims or Jesus the Baptists, no matter how they act, think or feel. Christians believe Christ will protect the Christians, no matter how they live and what they do. And the Jews hope for the coming of the Messiah in order to condemn the "bad" Arabs or Muslims and "pagan" Christians and to be rectified as "good" Jews. Everyone thinks that "their" God will take "their side" and destroy or condemn the others. Men still think that those who differ in creed or belief will be condemned! They think that studying Torah and being observant to the codex of halachic mitzvoth is enough to be rectified. Muslims think that praying at the mosques and declaring that "Allah is great" is enough to grant them eternal life and the Christians believe that if they believe and declare Christ as the only Son of God and the only Redeemer, they will automatically be saved. All of them have neither immersed themselves into the infinite ocean of divinity nor have they really become centers of light or compassion or led a life of selfless service for the sick or the poor, as all of the true saints, mahatmas, masters or real tzaddikim have done. They do not follow the shining examples of the masters in matters of lifelong self-discovery, service and purification, but simply think God will grant them redemption and resurrection because they speak their daily prayers, keep the mitzvoth, missionize in His name or simply because Christ has died on the cross and by this sacrifice redeemed them from their sins as long as they mentally believe and confess it.

Most people do not know or understand what such declarations really mean. Whether such dogmas, statements or teachings are true or not, we go astray if we do not go to their roots. Only if we discover their hidden meaning and totally eradicate our own will and little ego with all of their concepts, dogmas, pride, desires, bad habits, attitudes, beliefs and illusions through daily, deep, silent meditation, self-examination and self-submission can we say that we know God. The saints of all traditions have declared: "To know God means to become one with Him." And to become one with Him, Who is pure and eternal all-pervading consciousness and light, we have to submit, overcome and totally annihilate all of the aspects of our created personal identity. We have to die to all the mundane and personal expressions of the personal ego in order to merge into the infinite ocean of divine existence, consciousness and bliss, thus becoming a vessel and instrument of His infinite glory. Everyone who really merges into His ultimate Reality radiates His glory and His infinite virtues of eternal life and love; the individual mind dies, vanishes and the infinity of divine consciousness takes its place. It is our mind and egoistic personality that misleads and betrays us. God's will and plan is not to satisfy our minds and egos, but to replace them. We have to go out of our soul so that God can enter. The task of a seeker is not to polish his ego or to transform it into a "scholar" or a "believer," but to replace it, to empty his heart from all "I" and "mine" and allow God and His Holy Spirit to take its place.

Our deluded minds are not able to grasp the true, deep and hidden meaning of the holy scriptures in which all of the words and sentences point to the One Truth which is beyond word and thought. In order to grow spiritually, we need a God-realized preceptor, a God-intoxicated, pure and enlightened soul sent by His Majesty, the King of the Universe Himself. Only such a being who has divine vision can help us to become aware of our blind spots and delusions and has the power to awaken our sleeping spiritual essence. He can give us a taste of the Living God and an unforgettable experience of His infinite love and grace. That is the story of Job, who met different "scholars" or "believers" who wanted to give him advice. Then finally one came along who had achieved realization and the intervention of this Awakened One helped Job to "see" God, to really meet Him and experience His unspeakable compassion, fragrance and glory in his soul, heart and life. From then on Job stopped arguing and complaining because he had tasted Him. This taste calmed his mind and thoughts and saturated his painstruck and longing soul.

Because of a misguided or superficial understanding and interpretation of our scriptures, traditions and the "Word of God," we build walls and set separation between men and men, nation and nation, religious belief and religious belief. Due to very superficial interpretations and understandings, our minds grasp only the words and sentences and draw wrong conclusions. If our hearts were at least awake and open to the consequences of our misguided interpretations, we could feel the pain and cruelty we cause by them; these feelings of the heart would then stop us from causing separation and pain and call or force us to go deeper and become true seekers of the source and foundation of Truth itself. The ancient seers of the East were aware of this danger many thousands of years ago. They stated, "Ekam sat viprah bahudha vadanti," meaning: "There is only one Truth, but the sages have named it by different names." (Vedas).

We need to discriminate between essence and appearance, core and shell, surface and hidden depth. We cannot say, "I am Muslim" or "I am a Jew" and "therefore Allah or HaShem will take my side, rectify me or bless and protect my life and all of my undertakings." We rectify ourselves and argue as if there were two or even many Gods, i.e. Allah and HaShem, who are enemies, fighting with each other in order to show the whole world that we are the right and good people and that the others are wrong. We are so used to looking outside of ourselves, detecting the wrongs, faults and imperfections of others that we have become blind about ourselves.

Allah and HaShem are one. And since they represent but one reality, we could say it might be Allah who blesses the really devoted Jew, as it might be Adonai Zebaot who will shower the abundance of His grace upon the whole-hearted Muslim who truly yearns for Him and frees himself from passion and negative thoughts and emotions. And it might be Christ, understood as cosmic reality, that leads the purehearted Hindu or Jew or Muslim to resurrection and eternal life, while He, perhaps, keeps the proud, self-complacent and self-conceited Christian bound in suffering and darkness.

Allah, Adonai, Elohim, Brahman, Dharma, Nirvana or Tao are just but different names of the one, indivisible Ultimate Reality beyond mind and senses. All of the major religions have stated that truth of "There is but one God," "Ehamevam Advaititam," "Hu echad ve-ajin sheni," etc. God neither takes sides nor is He partial; He is all-embracing! The whole creation, lo, countless creations are embraced and contained within His superfluous Light, Love and life-giving Essence. He is all-permeating, the true core of all creations and creatures. He is the giver of breath to all, He is the sun that shines upon all of His creatures without any discrimination. He is the creator, origin, nourisher, goal and destination of all of us. He does not favor the angel over the worm or disfavor the Buddhist to the Jew. Everything has its place and is created to fill its particular place and purpose within the framework of God's plan, will and creation, according to its inborn divine essence, image and potential. And no sincere soul with a little bit of self-knowledge can or will claim any privilege or self-importance for himself, his breed or his people; he keeps a humble awareness of his incompleteness and imperfection in the face of the incomprehensible perfection and glory of God. If it is God's will to glorify, He will glorify and His glory will be visible before all the nations. But no one should glorify himself, except for fools or proud and blind souls.

Recently I heard a certain Rabbi in Jerusalem say, "Many Jews think that when the Messiah will come, he will tell them how right and good they are and have always been. But why do we then need a Messiah if we have always been images of perfection? Instead, I believe that when the Messiah comes, he will prove all of us to be wrong." I can fully agree with such a statement and it fits for Christians and Moslems as well. A God who takes sides or is partial is an invention of our deluded minds which are governed by pride and ego. Such a "God" is a projection of our unconscious lower nature which tries to deceive and lead us into the abyss of demonic self-destruction. God as the invisible but indestructible, beginningless root and origin of all existence neither favors nor disfavors, neither judges nor condemns. If the scriptures tell us that *He Who Is That He Is* would give favor to the just and condemn the wicked, they are using an anthropomorphism in order to point out the undeniable truth that all of our thoughts, attitudes and actions bear the fruit of consequences according to the law of cause and effect, which is also called the law of justice or the law of karma. It is not so that God becomes angry and comes to punish us; no,it is we ourselves who send out certain energies that then return to us and create pain, blindness, despair and suffering through their impure nature.

Saints and sages of all ages and traditions have witnessed and proclaimed this truth of an all-merciful, all-embracing God who does not exclude any creature from His life-giving grace and light. It is we who exclude or separate ourselves from Him and His replenishing waters. If we know His unlimited love and compassion and are aware of our own imperfection, our souls fill with true thankfulness, devotion and humility and we begin to see our fellow man and all of creation in a different light. We feel one with everything and all and start to experience cosmic consciousness, unity and joy. Soon we will even feel drunk with the wine of compassion and feel drawn to include and silently envelop all beings with this same joy, love and understanding as if they were members of our own body.

A man of God-realization becomes a mirror and vessel of God's purity and perfection. He no longer expresses personal thoughts, feelings or desires, but divine love, wisdom and selfless understanding. Being one with his Creator, he becomes a reflection of God's light and perfection. He humbly radiates love and light and all the shining rays of God's virtues. Since God is pure, he will behold purity; since God is Truth, he will behold Truth, and since God is all embracing, so his love and compassion will be all-embracing. Only one who manifests such divine qualities can be called a true Jew, a true Muslim or a true Christian. Neither Kabir nor Nanak (two Sufi saints), nor Zoroaster, nor Ramakrishna (a Hindu master), nor Meister Eckhart (a Christian mystic), nor Jeremiah (prophet of Israel), nor King David would have excluded or rejected any man or woman because of nationality, race, creed or belief. And if Moshe or Samuel collected the children of Israel, they did it for a special task and purpose and not because of personally preferring or favoring them over others.

Even God did not "favor" Israel, but had a "special" calling for them – in this there is a great difference. They were not the "better" people, but a people with a certain calling. Also Jesus, when he said, "I have come to save the fallen sheep of Israel" was only stating a special task of his mission; he never excluded any soul belonging to another nation, race or religious tradition. Mahatma Gandhi, when asked about his confession or religious belonging, simply answered: "I am Hindu, Muslim and Christian. I value the *Bhagavad Gita* (Hindu scripture) as highly as the *Gospels* and the *Qu'ran.*" And the Jewish sage and teacher of the Kabbalah (mystic lore of Israel), Max Mordechai Te'on became the preceptor and guru of many Christians and Arabs, as well as of the people belonging to his own flesh.

When Buddha started teaching he did not deny the divine origin of Rama or the teaching of Krishna, but simply worked and preached and awakened sleeping souls in order to restore justice and virtue (dharma) within a fallen and worldbound mankind. Ramakrishna proved the unity of religions in his own life through experiencing and practicing each of their innermost truths. He found that they all lead to the same ultimate goal and realization. Ramana Maharshi found the essence of Vedanta (Hindu spiritual tradition) perfectly expressed in the Books of Moses and the Psalms of David and stated that nowhere else had he found the vedantic truth of "Aham Brahmasmi," "Tat-twam-asi" or "Soham" so clearly stated as in the biblical revelation of God's being to Moses in the holy mantra, "Ehjeh Asher Ehjeh" or "I Am That I Am."

There would be no arguments of differences between Buddha or Christ, or Melkizedek or Zoroaster, or Moses and Mohammed, or Baal Shem Tow and Saint Frances of Assisi, or Al Hallaj and Saint Augustine, or Ramakrishna and Meister Eckhart. They are all made of the same essence, drinking of the same cup of wisdom and participating in the same one and indivisible Reality. They have all overcome their lower nature and all have raised their consciousness to the same lofty realm of divine existence. I have met saints, sages and tzadikkim of different religions and traditions and have found that they all respect one another and agree with each other; I have read the holy books of several religious traditions and found no divergence in the core and essence of their teachings. Of course they differ in terms of history, events, customs and rites, but their goals and paths of attainment are uniquely identical.

Also, different individuals or groups or even nations have or find different callings, tasks or missions within the great brotherhood of mankind, but they only discover, find and realize that special task or calling when they have gone deeply enough into self-discovery and gained closeness to God. One does not find one's calling or mission in books or through studies; one finds it only through deep meditation, self-discovery and by close encounter with God! This basic and elementary foundation of man's path to God is universal and it follows a universal law. Only the realization of one's vocation and task will reveal differences, but these will not cause separation or aversion between men or nations. God's plan leads to a wonderful unfoldment of individual patterns of tasks and missions that will not stand against each other but will complement and support one another like clogs in a clockwork. God created heaven and earth as a wonderful unity – everything is linked with everything else and each part has its counterpart in His creation. Within His great plan of perfection and realization we all are bound together.

In order to be wise, we have to leave the trodden paths of ignorant leaders and the dead, infertile, unconscious repeated dogmas, rites and rituals of the mediocre, self-conceited, self-complacent masses who seek self-rectification and comfort in their tradition, their churches, mosques and synagogues rather than in the lofty Light and Presence of our Living Lord and God. We should rather turn to and follow the saints, sages, masters and illumined souls who have struggled and succeeded in finding God and who, by their insight into the realm of the soul, can help us to remove our blindness and ignorance and guide us, by their luminous examples, along our paths. This would be far more helpful than listening to the dry or pathetic theologians, priests, scholars, imams, rabbis or preachers who have neither gained self-control nor self-knowledge, nor dispassion nor enlightenment and are, therefore, not able to bring forth a new light into our awareness and an essential change into our lives. Even if they have found a little light but not walked the whole way, they will mislead and misguide those who try to follow them. So, in the beginning, one should pray to God that He might have pity on us and send us a true and fully realized soul as a guide for our spiritual journey and a preceptor of eternal life.

So, my dear brothers and sisters, let us awaken and become aware of our divine and eternal birthright as children of God. Let us raise our hearts and minds to the infinite beauty of universal consciousness and breathe the air of spiritual realization. Let us lift our eyes to the horizons of the blazing light of a new age, elevate our souls and selves into the realm of lofty ideals and the bright light of pure self-knowledge. Let us all remember and live up to the truth of the Father and Mothership of God and all behave as true children of God who are bestowed with the divine inheritance of our heavenly Father-Mother-God that He-She has sown as a holy seed in our souls. Becoming aware of this radiant inheritance and divine potential as true children of Him, we will see, experience and treat each other as brothers and sisters and we will view and respect all of mankind as a great brotherhood of peace. Thus we will be living up to the eternal truth of our inborn godly nature, we will more and more manifest the divine qualities of His infinite spiritual being and we will embrace one another as God, our Father and Creator, embraces the whole of His creation with His infinite and unconditional love and existence.

II.

God-Realization: The Goal and Essence of all Spiritual Life

In our dark age even religious people or so-called "believers" are not aware of the lofty light or goal of religion and religious life. They think that being a "good" person, accepting and establishing certain beliefs and following the rules of their religion is enough for "attaining God." They believe, hope and imagine certain rewards in the hereafter and see death as the gate to final delivery and eternal life. "God-realization" is not even a word in their vocabulary, even less a goal to be envisioned or a state of awareness or consciousness to be reached within this short period of our earthly lives. Many imagine the goal of life to be a certain change in thoughts, beliefs and behaviors or the following of a certain pattern of thinking, believing and living which leads to a life in heaven where they will still continue to be individuals before God's throne or to a certain prophet or "deity" or master and those whom they loved in this earthly life.

All of these ideas may contain some truths, but they are infinitely far removed from the true heavenly goal and divine destiny of our lives and spiritual strivings. The goal is neither to remain as a separate individual entity or soul with its personal thoughts, imaginations, ideas or desires, nor to enter another etheric plane or world, the existence of which I do not want to deny. No, the goal is to reach a much greater attainment! It is the merging of our innermost spiritual essence and being into the infinite ocean of Divine Light, Consciousness and Bliss. With this as the goal, there remains no interest in identifying ourselves with any form of limited individuality, thought or plane of existence; there is only a most blissful awakened awareness of our identity in and with this transcendental Ultimate Reality which we call God and which is only to be found beyond the entities, qualities, names and forms of any created individuality or world (gross or subtle). Such a transcendental state of consciousness is beyond and above the three states of sleeping, dreaming or waking for the soul has become totally immersed and stabilized in divine unity with the cosmic cause. We call this "God-realization" because it is a continuous participation of our awareness in the One Infinite Cosmic Consciousness which is the core and self and light of all beings. It is not a mere change of mind or personality or a matter or way of thinking; it is the attainment of a totally different state of awareness and feeling which cannot be grasped by our minds. It can only be reached through total surrender of our mind and personality to the Divine Will and Presence of God and by raising our conscious awareness, together with a feeling heart, into His Holy Light.

A God-realized master or person, like Melkizedek, Lao Tzu, Ramakrishna, Buddha, Guru Nanak, Yogananda or Master Eckhart, is not someone who has gilded his ego or polished or sanctified his personality, but one who has reached a state of total annihilation of his ego and personality in order to merge into the sparkling ocean of Divinity. He has overcome his feeling of "I" and "mine," his attachment to mind and body and drowned himself in the light of pure consciousness. In the scriptures God reveals Himself as "I am an all-consuming fire." Someone who has fully surrendered to Him will find his little "i" consumed by the fire of God. His soul is flooded with God's infinite light, His fire of cosmic consciousness has entered his soul and taken the place of his little whiny ego so that he can truly say, "Not I, but God lives in me." The saints have stated, "I have died, but He has risen within me," and "I saw myself going out and Him entering the house." The Mahatmas have called it "Sahaja Samadhi," Buddha called it "Nirvana," the Vedas named it "Aham Brahmasmi" and the Torah has called it "I Am That I Am." It is difficult to explain how and what this state or experience really is since words cannot describe it; they can only point to it. Only if a little spark of this awareness has awakened within our soul, can we rise to some kind of feeling or intuitive understanding about what these words might denote.

The nature of God is both transcendental and immanent. He transcends all created worlds, whether gross or subtle, but is, at the same time, the root, cause and essence of all things and beings. This is also true of the consciousness and identity of a realized soul; its awareness, identity and love have become all-embracing. And since it has become aware of the illusive nature of its previous personal self and the whole universe, both of which are composed of the glamorous polarities created by temporary sense qualities, its consciousness and perception remain deeply rooted in pure transcendental self- awareness, beholding the appearance of this world as a projection of the all-creative power of this universal Consciousness onto its own screen. In this way, the whole flow of life, as well as the great stream of the changing appearances of this universe, are like a great multidimensional movie. And one of the "objects" or "actors" passing across the screen is this temporary personality, incarnate in a body made of flesh and bone, which one has identified with his own self.

The ancient sages and seers of India have called this wrong identification of the "self" with the "not self" or the mistaking of the "not-self" for the self, "Maya" or "the great delusion." They have discovered that the all-pervading, all-beholding and all-embracing universal consciousness which projects all of these myriad creatures and creation onto its own screen is the only Absolute Reality. *It Is That It Is.* The experience of oneness with It becomes the all-transcending experience of "I Am That I Am." Everything else, like ego, mind, self, personality, world or universe, has only transitory existence; they all have a beginning and what has a beginning also has an end.

Awakened to the one transcendental Consciousness, one finds oneself totally detached from mind and body and their sensations, feelings and pains. This does not mean that one is not aware of them, but that they are experienced only as pale shadows on the surface of the sea of Absolute Being, Consciousness and Bliss. At the same time our hearts, our intelligence and all of our faculties, like reasoning, sensing, moving, smelling and tasting, are doing their work and service in this relative world but are no longer led by the whims and desires, concepts and imaginations, ideas and projections of our personalities, egos or individual wills. They are guided by the one wisdom-guided will and plan of God. This does not mean that our individuality is annihilated or destroyed; no, the individuality remains but we do not experience an identification with it. We experience only universal, divine self-awareness as our true self and being and see individuality as one of the infinite instruments for expressing this one universal consciousness.

It is this consciousness, called God, which cares for all the jewels of individualities and beholds them in His universal mind and memory. It is He who takes all of these forms and moves them about on the screen of life. He is the Creator and Mover of all things; He is the one life of all created beings and the one light and self of all of us. If and when we have shaken off the delusive bonds of our blind little selves and minds, we will become aware of Him as the One Living Being who abides in all these names and forms, the very Self of our selves and the Light of our lights. And, as I said above, we will experience all these selves and bodies as our own self and body! The joy of one of them will be the joy of all of us and the pain of one of them will be our pain. Yet both, individual pain as well as collective pain, will be carried and comforted by the light, peace and joy absolute that are rising from the unreachable depth of God, from the infinite Source of all sources, from the bottom of the one all-pervading Self of all selves.

Speaking of this true state of selfhood, one or the other of us might resign, saying "I will never reach nor even get a glimpse of such a state." My dear friend and companion on this journey from physical birth to death:

never resign nor falsely postpone your spiritual striving for realization! Never forget the unlimited power and unspeakable grace of divinity which so easily is able and willing to break the chains of our bondage and lift the veils of our blindness. A look into the realm of divine life should not leave us untouched or undecided; it should rather set us on fire, should awaken and inspire us to stand up from our graves and rise to our true identity. We should not put or draw the high ideals of life down into our lowliness, but rather climb out of our darkness and strive for the one attainment that is of unspeakable peace and joy and which lifts us to immortality and eternal universal life. No earthly joy can be compared with this inner state of serenity and grounding. Of course it needs true aspiration, a humble heart, strength of decisiveness, the ability to discriminate illusion from reality, the transitory from the eternal, the willingness to renounce self and its attachments and endurance in our inner struggle. And there can be no greater blessing than finding a relaxed soul appointed by God who accepts us as a disciple, guiding us with great care and understanding and deep affection of heart to this attainment.

Really putting our foot upon such a path of realization will not bring instant enlightenment, but it will bear instant fruit. It will give us the unfailing feeling of meaning and direction, will sharpen our awareness and sense of care in every field and aspect of our lives and will establish a new and more vivid relationship to God and our fellow beings, altogether bringing more peace and confidence into our hearts and minds. On the way to conscious spiritual realization we will find God Himself working an incredible miracle. While striving to overcome our identification with our little self and ego, in order to raise our awareness from the level of the individual to the level of universal consciousness, we will experience a slow but absolutely miraculous unfolding of our true God-given individuality. This will be born and slowly revealed in forms of pure self-expression on the one side, and as true vocation on the other. Both are linked together like the two sides of one coin.

The more clear and unfaltering the ways are that we find to express the stream of life and love flowing from above though our hearts and minds, the more clearly we find our way to our true vocations. Many of our potentials, which until then were covered and hidden, become visible and our feelings towards self, life, people, profession and environment change until we find ourselves strangely drawn to a special task or service within this world. All of these changes take place through becoming true to our inborn nature and, at last, God awakens special potentials within ourselves and opens new gates of experiences and possibilities leading to a life of service and full self-realization. Within such a life of service, abiding in our vocation, we will attain the unfolding and realization of our God-given gifts, potentials and true individuality. The soul is like a seed that will grow into a giant tree in the garden of humanity if it is placed in the fertile ground of correct service and self-expression. It can also be compared to a tiny spark of divine light conditioned to expand to a sparkling star, radiating its luminosity from the heavens of enlightment into the dark night of spirital ignorance.

Continuous self-discovery, devotion to God and selfless service to Him and mankind are the three indispensable pillars of the noble path of God-realization. Self-discovery is the inward-drawn use of the discriminatory power of our conscious perception which helps us to eliminate all wrong identification and thus penetrate through all the layers of our mind to dive into the ground of our true being. Whatever thought, image, emotion or desire might arise, we put it aside by the conscious consideration that all these reactions are nothing but waves on the surface of our true being. We leave them aside and try to discover the one essence beyond all thoughts, sense impressions, emotions and desires which is the root of our discriminatory power itself. We ask: "Who am I? What is my true being? What is the immortal essence of all the changing phenomena of my consciousness? Who is it that is listening within me? Who is it that is witnessing all the thoughts and images that pass before the screen of my awareness? Who is it that is the seer and the perceiver of all these transitory things outside or inside of my mind?" If we really answer these questions in our depths, we will become aware that we are neither this mortal body nor this limited mind. This work of inner discrimination and elimination of what is not true self, but illusory personal identity, is self-discovery. It is done and achieved not by our reasoning or thinking, but by discriminatory conscious perception directed to its own root.

Developing devotion to God, though, is the work of our heart. Directing all of our feelings, our longings, our love, our pain and our joy to the heart of God and surrendering all of our dreams, desires and emotions to His Will is true devotion. Praying to God with a burning heart, accepting and bringing all the pains and injustices that we experience to the feet of our Lord is devotion. Such heartfelt devotion, which makes us shed thousands of tears, tears of desperate longing, of pain due to separation from Him, pain about all our weaknesses, our heartlessness, our blindness, our selfishness and tears of love and joy, will open and transform our lonesome hearts which are hardened and armored by pride, egocentric will and all those selfish thoughts which arise in our "I-and-mine" centered minds.

Such devotion melts our hearts and makes them humble, soft and loving. Devotion and meditation ally us with both strength and love. They lead to the surrender of our selfish will and ego and bring our mind under the reign of the qualities of our purified heart. Self-discovery first achieves awareness of our impurities, failures and imperfections before leading to self-realization. It brings light onto our lowliness and humiliates our pride. In deep, devoted prayer we bring all these impurities and imperfections before God; we lay them before His feet, pouring out our hearts which ache with the pain of repentance and love so that we may receive His compassionate touch which purifies and comforts our hearts. Self-discovery and devotion go hand-in-hand; self-discovery without devotion freezes into stagnation and devotion without self-discovery ends in blind romantic feelings. Both have to accompany each other.

The heart is the center of our life and therefore has to be the center of our spiritual path. In fact, the heart is the place of our inner struggles, striving and achievement. Most of us have first to find our hearts which are buried under many layers of dullness or walls of selfish separation. Without deep feelings we can neither pray nor love, see nor understand, exercise softness nor forgive and we cannot find compassion. Without an open heart we do not see the needs and sorrows of our fellow men or sense the closeness of the presence of God; without a feeling heart, we are dead to the joys and achievements of spiritual life. Without a loving heart we are not even awakened to our human nature and calling.

So the transformation, purification and melting of our hearts is the first task on our spiritual path. The heart is not only the seat of our feelings but also of our true individuality, our awareness and our inborn divinity. These all have their seat in our heart and it is, therefore, impossible to develop love, awareness, individual potential or even God-consciousness without discovering and transforming our heart.

The third pillar on the path to God-realization is an attitude of selflessness in all of our activities. Selflessness does not mean denial of our basic needs or living conditions, but the surrender of our selfish interests to a universal selfless ideal. If we have such an attitude that places the universal ideal first, we also will find that our own needs become satisfied and fulfilled. This attitude of selflessness in our actions not only purifies our hearts and minds, but also leads to pure self-expression and, last but not least, to the discovery of our divine task and vocation which is imbedded within our individuality and seated in the core of our heart.

This individuality, which can be identified with a pure and sparkling crystal or diamond, if activated and purified in the light of self-awareness, functions as a vessel of the Light of Divine Consciousness. It can be compared to a precious stone housing a spark or source of light that radiates from its center outwards through its transparent body. This light becomes refracted by the facets of the stone's cut and shines forth into the surrounding space. Such a crystal, with its specific shape or cut, represents the shape, form or self-expression of our God-given individuality, while the light within can be compared to the pure consciousness abiding therein. Using this image we gain a clear view into our true nature. While, as individual beings, we are all "made" of the same crystalline substance of precious stone, the cut of our stones differs widely from others. Each stone, while made of the same material, shows a different shape and form and also a different display of light. Through the help of this example we can understand that each and everyone of us, even when purified from pride, selfishness and ego, will differ in his or her self-expression, such as in his or her smile or gait or gestures. Nevertheless, we also see that it is the same life and light that flows, shines and radiates through all of us, enlightening the space around us. This light that flows through all of us is the divine life and light of God. As there is only one light but many colors, there is only one consciousness and life but many conscious living beings. They differ in "shape" and "form", but all participate in and radiate the same singular light of God. In this way Buddha, Krishna, Moses or Jesus differ in voice, language, walk or gesture, but all of them radiate the same light, express the same truth and manifest the same holy presence of God. In the same way, everyone of us, if really purified to the core of our being, beholds, manifest and radiates the same universal light and awareness even though it is broken according to the specific cut of our inborn individuality.

This individuality is not fully manifest or awake in the seeking soul. It rather lies dormant in the depth of our soul, waiting to be awakened in order to unfold and show its hidden gifts and potentials. In fact, the individuality can be compared to a tiny little spark or seed of light sown by God into the unlimited space of His infinite being. Covered with several sheaths or subtle bodies, it starts its journey through this universe.

God Himself is the ground into which it is sown to live, grow and bear fruit. Just like every other seed which carries the image of its fully grown organism within itself, so the spark of our individuality carries the God-like image of its fully-realized potential within itself. Just as the mustard seed carries the image of a mustard tree and the chestnut seed the image of a huge chestnut tree within themselves, so also do each of us carry the image of a fully grown God-man within ourselves. That is why a Chassidic master used to say that he was not supposed to become an Abraham or Moses, but to become himself. And we recall the ancient saying, “Man, become what your are.” In this manner, everyone is designed and destined to become himself, to unfold his dormant potential as an individual human being and God-man. And just as a seed must break in order to grow into a tree, to blossom and to bear fruit, so too is man destined to allow his outer mask to be broken so that he can give birth to his inner individuality with all of its gifts and potential. In this way we slowly develop into a huge Tree of Life, rooted in the soil of eternal existence, bringing forth blossoms of heavenly gifts and fruit of divine virtue.

We know that each developed tree reveals and manifests the divine essence and entity from which its seed stems from. As the seed of a peach tree will become a peach tree and the seed of an almond tree will become an almond tree, so the seed of God will grow to a son or daughter of God, finally becoming a God! Such an unfoldment and realization, though, is granted only through a spiritual life that is modeled according to our true inner nature. We have to live up to our inborn divinity and start to express divine qualities in order to bring this sleeping potential to birth. As long as we express only low and impure qualities, we suffocate this dormant holy spark in us, mutilate it and disfigure our inborn God-like image. So many people would even rather lower their true nature to the level of a rational, egotistical animal or a demon instead of becoming what they are destined to be.

The path to such a high ideal of God-realization is to live a conscious, spiritual life based on three pillars: self-discovery, deep devotion to God and a selfless attitude in our actions. Self-discovery represents the light, devotion to eternal truth the water and selflessness in action the forces of the soil and the seed which cause it to grow into a tree. If we model our lives on these ageless truths, which correspond to the truth and nature of our true self, our lives will become rich, filled with inner peace and joy and be blessed with the fruits of spiritual immortality and eternal life. May God be the caring gardener who bestows our souls with Divine Light and heavenly waters; may He touch our eyes to make us see and our hearts to awaken us to true aspiration and love, enabling us to make our way to the peak of our destination and our lofty calling. Amen.

III.

The Two Aspects of Truth and Religion

Like every other created thing and being, each one of us experiences a twofold origin and identity. On the one hand, we find our ultimate identity in the Absolute Being of God; on the other, in our God-given "name" or individuality. Adhering only to the first, we ultimately reach an awareness of all-encompassing and all-embracing unity. While we are on the way to that realization, we also witness the miracle of the unfoldment of the tiny seed of our divine individuality which reaches its expression in the course of discovering our true vocation, as described before in chapter two.

Through this two-fold origin and identity we discover that we are one by our universal light, but differentiated by our past deeds, our vocation and our individuality. This is not only true for individual souls but also for spiritual groups and whole nations. We will find that every individual, according to its preconditions (Pravabda) and its state of realization, is more or less rooted in a specific tradition and that every spiritual group or folk belongs to a special heritage which originally was initiated by a specific avatar or messenger of God. So we find that many authentic spiritual groups follow a special rule of discipline initiated by the founder of the group but, nevertheless, all share the same light, brotherly love and vision of indivisible unity.

In the same way, we find whole nations like India, China, ancient Egypt, Israel or Ishmael having their own specific spiritual or religious inheritance which they are struggling to rediscover so as to find their true identity. It is only fanatic misunderstanding, caused by spiritual ignorance and egotism, that leads to the sicknesses and plagues of hatred and destruction that we see now everywhere in the world. In fact, the abysses and hatreds that so deeply split and antagonize mankind today are based on religious fanaticism and misguidedness. Since religious questions touch the deepest nerves of our existence, their misunderstanding and misinterpretation cause the deepest pains and splits.

All of the enmities and wars we witness today in our world have their roots in blind demands for exclusive access to, possession of and control over some of the values, objects or sites of religious inheritance. It is the demand for special privileges, rights or even of superiority and the claim to possession of the only truth or exclusive control over temples or holy sites that are the roots of all of the tensions between Muslims and Hindus in India and Pakistan, as well as between Christians and Jews and Muslims in Israel and other places in our western world. Jews and Arabs both demand exclusive access and control of the Temple Mount and the City of Jerusalem; Christians and Jews struggle with each other for ages over the question of messiahship and redemption and all three of them claim to be in possession of the "one" truth, each preaching that they are the only "true" heirs and "advocates" of God! What a crazy world!

Instead of applying the noble truths and values of our own tradition to our own lives and learning from helping, serving and loving one another in the acknowledgment of the One Fatherhood of God, we fight, humiliate, terrorize and destroy each other, exploiting our very souls and our inheritance for the sake of obliteration.

How much more religious it would be to respect the differences and diversifications within mankind, among the big family of human beings, as we do within the rest of this incomprehensible creation. Many problems arise because of our tendency to compare ourselves with others. Many destructive evaluations and judgments which arise out of this tendency lead to different forms of irrational likes and dislikes, to antagonisms and to divisions amongst us, all based on comparisons of sex, race, nationality, language or creed. We need not only to learn to accept these miraculous varieties amongst us, but to lovingly embrace and enjoy them just like we enjoy a bouquet of diversified flowers brought forth from the infinitely creative bosom of Mother Nature. All faculties, virtues, gifts, abilities, inabilities, all the differences of nationality, race, sex, temper and individuality which manifest in body and mind arise from the indivisible source and creative Word of God. They are like the whole spectrum of colors which spring forth and merge back into the oneness of light. The whole creation is like a huge cosmic tree of differentiation, growing and unfolding from that one source of life that is rooted in the absolute being of the Creator.

If we become aware of the fact that all the variety of qualities and qualifications, as well as the continuous changes in things, creatures and life (more concretely speaking of the differences in all things and creatures according to destiny, individuality and the course of life) are not concerned with the divine essence but with the outer appearance on the surface of phenomenological existence, we will feel and understand that one can by no means compare oneself with any other created thing or being except God. If we become conscious of this, we will feel and understand that we cannot apply the same measures to different individuals or situations. Everything is distinct by itself through its appearance, but is inseparably one with God. Abiding by this truth, one will find oneself in a condition of detachment and unceasing marvel about the fathomless beauty of the ungraspable variety of names and forms constantly moving upon and passing over this stage of space and time, on the screen of consciousness. One will learn to see perfection in everything and if the question of lack of perfection arises, one will seek for the roots of imperfections in one's own mind and attitudes first.

Seeing the essential oneness of creation and knowing the origin and cause of variety, two aspects which are contained in the very core of all religious teachings, one develops true humility and respect towards all and everything and restrains from any form of possessiveness towards any religious or spiritual good or value, as well as from any claim for superiority in relation to values, revelations or traditions. One will not exclude anyone who is truly aspiring for liberation, purification, self-perfection and God-realization from access to such spiritual goods and values, unless he proves unworthy through a lack of truthfulness, respect or ethical conduct in life. In this way one improves in his own striving, not only by applying the teachings of his own tradition but also by respecting and learning from others. Furthermore, one enjoys being at peace with every being and enjoys close relationships with all people, independent of their national, racial, religious or spiritual background or their different individuality or task. With such a basis of understanding, respect and brotherly love, we can and will victoriously march toward the realization of a brotherhood of peace and God's kingdom on earth.

Truth and religion always have two aspects. One is the universal aspect, based on the unity of God as the one indivisible reality and His laws which immanently guide and govern our lives and the totality of this creation. The second is specific, based on the different individual purposes, callings, situations, stages and historic conditions of individuals, groups or even whole nations. Based on these, the different religions deal, on the one side, with the universal law and nature of God Himself, the universal purpose, law and destination of life, man and creation, the universal nature and condition of our hearts, minds and souls as well as with the laws, conditions, steps and stages of our paths towards full realization. On the other hand, they also cope with the specific vocations, tasks, needs and conditions in relation to the apparent differences due to time, space and individual conditions. In these matters we have to be aware that the universal aspect and the vision of unity are always superior and of higher value than the specific or individual. The common origin, ground, purpose, essence and goal of all our lives is the Fatherhood of God and it is of much higher order and value than the phenomenal, historic and individual differences which mark only the peripheral existence of ourselves. Any open-hearted, open-minded soul would, therefore, always adhere to the Light that we have in common instead of focusing on the outer differences that separate us. It is important that we always surrender the individual to the universal and that we see the One in the many, unity in diversity, God in each and every individual. He that is beyond name and form, beyond time, space, history and diversification is the light, the truth, the life and essence of all of us. He brings forth diversity as a tremendous play or fireworks, as a cosmic unfolding of His creative and projecting power upon the screen of His consciousness.

Every religion and religious tradition encompasses different fields of subjects according to the different quests and aspects of human life. In our basic quest for meaning, we ask for the who, what, why, when and how of life. These questions apply to the subject of our search, who is God, to the object of our search which is man, to the condition of life which is the world, to the process of time which is history, to the cause which is the search for the law, and to the how which is the search for the answer and solution or the practical approach we have to take in order to adequately respond to the great and unique quest of life. According to these different questions, the religious systems embrace different aspects of teaching and tradition, such as:

- theology: the science and knowledge of God,
- cosmology: the science of the origin, the structure, the course, the goal and the meaning of creation,
- anthropology: the science of the origin, the place, the

nature, the goal and the meaning of the human being within creation,
- history: the science of the course and destiny of mankind and its different peoples,
- metaphysics: the science of the cosmic spiritual laws that govern the course of the universe and of our lives, like the law of cause and effect,
- ethics: the science of the inner mental and behavioral conditions of well-being with oneself and with each other,
- psychology: the science of the laws, the faculties, the powers, the aspects and the conditions of the human mind and psyche,
- tradition: a compendium of symbols, legends, stories, forms and rites, feasts and ceremonies etc. of outer-directed religious life, including liturgy, sacramental acts, biographies of saints, etc. and
- mysticism: the science of the ultimate destiny and goal of human life, the path of its realization and its practical approach.

We can, in fact, see nine different disciplines within each body of religion. Each religion has an exoteric, that is to say a mainly outwardly-oriented or directed approach, and an esoteric or inwardly-oriented approach. While the exoteric is mainly to be understood as an educational tool for the mass of people who have not awakened to a psychological and spiritual awareness, the esoteric approach is meant for the few who are receptive to and willing to follow a spiritual calling. While the border between the exoteric and esoteric approaches is a fluid one and runs straight through the disciplines of theology, cosmology, anthropology, history and ethics, tradition is put mainly onto the side of the exoteric and metaphysics, psychology and mysticism on the side of the esoteric. While the unawakened person lacks a conscious awareness of the inner dimension of life and thereby only has access to the exoteric level or to the traditional approach towards religion, the awakened person gains access to the esoteric level which deals with the invisible and intangible reality of inner life as well as with the relationship to God, the world and the self in totality. Thus, the masses are taught in terms of rules, commandments, symbols, rites, stories and analogies in order to culturally, mentally and psychologically enrich and ethically anchor their lives, while the more psychologically responding and receptive souls are guided on the narrow path of the esoteric approach towards inner transformation, enlightenment and spiritual self-realization.

In our present time we can see that a most powerful spirit of awakening is blowing through this deeply sleeping world, shaking its foundations in order to bring forth a higher and more conscious awareness concerning the quest for meaning in our lives. Through this, the division between the sleeping majority and the waking minority is slowly being shifted. We are living in an era where the mere traditional approach of religion has become more of an obstacle to peace and spiritual realization than an aid. Only a new spirit of self-awareness which leads us through the narrow gate of esoteric self-discovery will help us to escape a total disintegration of mankind. The technological achievements of the worldwide intercommunication of our present age have, at least on a technical level, brought the ends of this world much closer together, this being a part of divine providence bringing about a new spirit of international exchange and cooperation and speeding up the process of spiritual development, interreligious understanding and reconciliation throughout the world.

We need to awaken and stand up to our true and divine inner nature and to stop declaring self-made ideas and imaginations of our gods. It is time to begin to discover the all-permeating spirit of the living God that is not a mere imagination, but the very breath and essence of our soul-life, of our self and I. He, that is the Self of selves and the I of I's, who is closer to our soul than we ourselves, has to rise into the focus of our awareness. In order to let this happen, we have to direct our awareness inwardly towards the core of our feeling heart and touchable receptive being. Only there will we discover the eternal truth and meaning of our religion and existence.

Since the exoteric approach is dealing more with the outer phenomenal aspects of life and creation, it is subject to many phenomenal and historic differences. The esoteric, on the other hand, is by nature more closely in touch with the inner essence and is, to a great extent, more all-comprehensive and universal. It is involved with the nature of God, the nature of the world and the mind, the ethical, cosmological and psychological laws of life in general and their practical application on our paths to God and God-realization.

The exoteric is always specific and, if misunderstood, separating and divisive. The esoteric, on the other hand, is mainly universal and therefore reconciling, unifying and all-embracing. Those subjects of esoteric religion that are not universal but specific, such as the callings of Ishmael and Israel, are put under a light of much deeper understanding and vision and thus lifted to a level of awareness that is far beyond evaluative judgment or discrimination and, therefore, accessible to a general understanding and discussion beyond mystification, emotional statements and argumentation.

In summarizing, we can see that the esoteric approach of religion is always concerned with the universal core of religious quest which is beyond phenomenal specification and discrimination. Its goal is to discover and illuminate the secrets of the essence of our being. It also includes the revelation and explanation of the invisible hidden causes of the phenomenal differentiations, as far as they are essential to the understanding of our spiritual quest. Everything that is not essential to spiritual realization drops and is left behind, similar to an unpleasant weight being dropped when we try to climb the peak of a mountain.

So now we understand and have a practical tool that we can use for examining and investigating religions for their relevant and true cores; we have to purify them from all man-made attributes and additions and reduce them to their untouchable body of eternal and divine truth. It is not scholarly interpretations but revelations and insights received by illumined minds which lead to truth. That is originally what is meant by the words "Kabbalah" (receiving) or Sufism (haqiqa). Only such knowledge and teaching can lead aspiring souls to the mountain peaks of liberation, cosmic love and spiritual perfection.

As was mentioned before, we need a new spirituality instead of remaining in sleep and dreaming in the nice beds of man-made institutional religious traditions and beliefs. We need spiritual experience and knowledge of the divine instead of dogmas, orthodoxy and mere mental beliefs and speculations. Only a living vision of God can change us and make us religious in a deeper spiritual way. It is only the true esoteric approach that can lead us to enlightenment and sanctification. What we primarily need is a universal approach towards God and spiritual life; we need a spiritual understanding of the nature, the structure and the working of our minds and psyches, of our egos and personalities and a growing awareness of the nature and essence of our soul as the abode of divine light and consciousness. Secondly, we need a profound knowledge and understanding of the laws of inner transformation as well as of the steps, tests, dangers, possible pitfalls, signposts, experiences, aids and spiritual foundations of our path to enlightenment and spiritual attainment. Only thirdly might it be necessary and useful to deal with more specific questions of religious tradition and theology. Such questions and issues only arise in relation to specific facts or experiences concerning the karmic patterns of past lives or individual questions of our calling and vocation. These facts, experiences or insights might reveal a concrete relationship or belonging to or certain tasks towards a specific tradition or place. If this is the case, we have to know from the very beginning that such an inclusion is always only of a temporary character. We might discover ourselves being rooted in the cradle of eastern or western tradition and through that understand the relevance of specific prophetic revelations or messages to our personal lives. If so, we then have to implement these religious messages or prophetic revelations to our own lives.

We may even learn to understand the relevance of eastern or western or even more specific traditional lore for our own path. We might find our own destiny connected and interwoven with the destiny of China or ancient Egypt, with "Jacob" or "Ishmael" or even a very definite tribe or spiritual group. If such facts or questions arise, we have to remember that they are essentially of temporary character. As we have to overcome our personal identification, we also have to overcome the identification with any specific tribe or tradition and finally realize our ultimate identity with the universal being of God, the pure consciousness of "I AM", beyond any attributes or qualifications. Nowhere else can we find liberation, eternal life and unconditional love, bliss and peace. If we really and undoubtedly find ourselves conditioned by our individuality and belonging to a certain definite tradition, then we have to, of course, deal with it and fulfill our temporary task that is linked with such an association. We also have to know that such questions are the very root of many confusions and problems, leading to seemingly unbridgeable splits between individuals, groups, peoples and nations throughout mankind in this world today. Lacking an enlightened vision of life, such questions and their unenlightened answers can cause many errors and easily lead us astray. Here we need not only to have a deep vivid esoteric vision and understanding, but also the help of an enlightened guide or mentor who can safely guide us through the jungle of misconceptions, imaginations and emotional traps. It is important that we at least remember the following: first, we are human beings and children of God and only secondly do we belong to a specific tradition, nation or group.

But let us return to the question of pure spiritual religion. In looking upon it we have found three pillars of such an approach, the first two being really fundamental and indispensable for our spiritual path. Calling them by name, we find them to be:

- esoteric psychology or the psychology of mind, psyche and self-understanding, combined with a universal approach of ethics and
- scientific mysticism, based on profound metaphysics.

Both of these are purely universal. Esoteric psychology, scientific mysticism and metaphysics are absolutely universal, in theory as well as in their practical application. They are not conditioned through any geographic, national or historic specifications. Even if our mentalities vary on a wide scale, the minds of a Chinese, a Sikh, a Muslim, a Christian or a Jew are essentially of the same nature, ruled and operating by the same universal laws. The same is true for the patterns of spiritual unfoldment and realization and the stages of the path of initiation. They are all governed by a universal law. Since God, life and creation are one and we all are nothing but manifestations and individualizations of His divine consciousness and light, this principle of universal validity of esoteric psychology and scientific mysticism is to be easily understood. There is nobody exempt from these universal laws.

If we follow this insight and really adhere to this truth, we cannot but accept and welcome the idea of the universal validity, applicability and interchangeability of these subjects within and between all religious traditions. By that we can understand the Vedic quote: "Ekam sat viprah bahudha vadanti," - there is but one Truth, although the sages have called it by many names. The Sufi master, the Christian saint, the Hindu yogi or the Jewish kabbalists will share the same universal insights, the same virtues and the same transcendental experiences. They all will understand the unique and indisputable language of love and silence and adhere to the same cosmic truth. If they really have attained cosmic consciousness, there will not even be one tone of discord or one note of disharmony amongst them. It is only the followers and aspirants that might disagree or dispute about the questions of this unconditional truth and eternal life springing from it. But if they will learn to humble themselves in the awareness of their clouded minds and spiritual ignorance, they will learn to respect and love each other and by deep common study and meditation will immensely learn and benefit from each other. It is important to realize that we can share and exchange the great spiritual achievements of the different traditions and benefit from each other without having to be afraid of getting caught or mixed up in specific customs, rites or dogmas which are born of ambitious imaginations, of mere intellectual theologians or colorful fantasies of oriental storytellers.

Altogether we should sharpen our awareness to and enjoy the fact that the different nations and traditions are meant to complement and enrich each other just as the organs of our body complement each other and depend on another in their tasks and operations within the functioning of the body as a whole. Every tradition has brought forth glorious highlights in different fields of initiatic science. It is through the great immortal sages, saints and seers of all ages that mankind is blessed not only by illuminating insights into the realm of eternity and the joys of divine life, but also by most minute and lucid introductions, guidelines or tracts which have cast light onto all questions and dimensions of the spiritual path.

Some of these tracts or guidelines of imponderable value are the *Yoga Sutras* of Maharishi Patanjali, the *Dhammapada* of Gautama Buddha, the *Viveka Chudamani* of Sri Shankara, the writings of the *Philokalia* of the early desert fathers in Egypt, Palestine, Syria and Greece, the *Bhakti Sutras* of Narada, the *Bhagavad Gita* of Vyasa Rishi, the essential teachings of Vedanta and the *Upanishads*, the immortal writing of some of the great masters of Sufism like Gelal-ad-Din Rumi (*All and One*), Ibu Arabi with his *Fusus-al-hikam* or *Ruh-al-quds*, Al Ghazali, Mansur al-Hallaj, Attar or Kabir, the works of Plato, Plotin, Meister Eckhart or Juan de la Cruz and last but not least, of some of the great kabbalists and Chassidic masters of old, such as Isaak Luria, Moshe Chayim Luzzatto or Chayim of Voloczyn. Of course we could find and mention many, many more of them, even down to our present day. All of these works and masters share an absolutely universal vision of spiritual life and the path of

God-realization. They are not caught up with specific religions or their institutional doctrines but are exclusively concerned with the universal dimensions of our eternal quest for God and self-realization. These scriptures are not the exclusive possession of isolated groups or sects but the most luminous treasures of entire mankind. As souls of universal vision, the authors of these scriptures and teachings were drawing from the unlimited source of divinity and illumination, following their concern with the destiny of mankind as a whole and the human search for liberation from bondage and darkness in general.

Of course there are many, many more scriptures or compendia of teachings and even living realized masters in our days, but here we have mentioned only those of universal concern and validity for the serious spiritual seeker on his path. Many of the other books or scriptures of tradition, like the Hindu *Puranas*, the *Torah* of the Israelites, the texts of the Jewish prophets or the *Quran*, deal with many subjects of mainly specific, historic or even local concern; therefore, they have to be understood in a different light. I am not saying that they are of less importance or less value or of a lower origin; sometimes even the opposite might be true, but they deal with God's plan with a distinct people, tribe or nation, with a specific historic dimension of their destiny, inheritance or vocation and are, therefore, in these aspects, necessarily restricted to these distinct cases or conditions. This should be well understood.

Searching and looking for an understanding of the universal laws and foundations of our spiritual life and path, of inner transformation, purification, sanctification, illumination and final liberation, we have to draw and learn from the unique treasures of the universal initiatic teachings of world scriptures and world traditions. If we open our hearts and minds to this simple fact and start to study these great works of mysticism, metaphysics, esoteric psychology and ethics, or the commentaries and interpretations of them by the illumined masters of our time, we will find guidance of imponderable value. Often only the more detailed introduction to and explanation or expounding of these teachings by a contemporary spiritual master will open the gates for the correct understanding and application of them in our daily lives. All of us can easily find access to the sources of such perennial wisdom and knowledge, but only through an enlightened teacher or messenger of God will we be able to apply them to our spiritual discipline and exercise in order to realize their goals and harvest the fruit of eternal life.

We have acknowledged now three steps of preparation for finding our path: the first is the study of holy books in order to understand the basic principles of the spiritual path, the second is intense and wholehearted prayer for guidance and redemption and the third is the search for a realized master who will guide us through this adventure of self-discovery, spiritual discipline and "God-intoxicated" life. If we are well prepared and inwardly ripe, the teacher will come. If we follow him, he will illuminate our minds with an entirely new understanding which will lead our souls to new dimensions of inner experience and love; he will, finally, raise our consciousness and heart to the sphere of ultimate unity and peace. On the course of such a path we will taste the bliss of self-realization and the sweetness of God and touch the very root of the universe and all things; therefore, we do not need any theology or cosmology or even anthropology because through self-realization we will receive and experience or envision our own theology and cosmology firsthand within the inner chamber of our heart. As the Oracle of Delphi of old states: "Know thyself and thou shalt see God and the cause of the universe (within yourself)."

To summarize: What is true spirituality and religion? Everything that helps us to realize God, which means to gain self-understanding, to purify our hearts and minds, to develop unconditional love and compassion, virtue, selflessness and humility, to reach perfection, to attain cosmic consciousness and to meet God face-to-face is true religion. It is important not to "discuss" religion or to judge or evaluate which one is "the best", but to realize their common ideals. Utilize the best of all religions for the best of humanity and yourself. Realize your true Self which is infinite joy and bliss, impeccable purity and light, tranquillity, serenity, peace, universal love and immortality. Most of the present religious traditions will disappear and will be replaced by higher teachings and higher truths. "Out of Zion will come a new teaching and out of Jerusalem will come the Word of God" (Micah).

Many mentally trapped people think that "Torah" only means the Torah of Moses, but God does not stop to give new revelations. In fact, the story of life is a permanent revelation leading us from stage to stage unto a final reabsorption of this entire creation into its origin and source. All religions are only aids or schools revealed and given according to the needs and evolutionary state of the people. During our evolutionary development we pass through different stages and states. It is similar to a child that is growing in understanding and skill, who passes from kindergarten to primary school and then through the different grades to maturity and on to the university. The Mosaic laws can be compared to the kindergarten or first grade of spiritual understanding and realization; they help to tame the animal within us and to bind the "yetzer ha-ra," but are not clearly pointing out the path to mystic realization and final liberation. They establish a minimal condition in regard to ethical conduct and purity but do not expound on the path to ultimate spiritual perfection and cosmic consciousness.

Of course the born mystic, having developed a deep intuitive understanding through many incarnations, will find the "summum bonum" of the esoteric truth in the simple statement, "I Am That I Am." But the seeking soul standing at the portal of inner awakening will not be able to find the necessary guidance in mere exoteric religion or mosaic law. The quest for higher realization requires a much more detailed understanding of the working of our minds and psyches. The seeker has to leave the trodden path of institutional exoteric religion and start to search for the hidden, the intangible, the transcendental. He has to discover his own Self and reach out for the pure spiritual realm of life and God Himself. It is necessary to transcend the physical, sensual and mental levels and to dive deeply into the vast sea of pure feeling, consciousness and light. It is only through the higher knowledge of initiatic science which provides us with the spiritual tools and weapons necessary for the investigation and conquest of the unknown space of our soul which, for a long time, was only accessible to the chosen few and only recently, in the pangs of a new era, is moving into the reach of many, that we will be enabled to enter the gateways of a spiritual path. Only through the study of metaphysics, esoteric psychology and scientific mysticism as revealed and taught by the great masters of our spiritual world tradition, who themselves succeeded in their struggles and conquered the crown of immortality, will we find profound direction and guidance for our own spiritual search and discipline. These masters of divine life are the only true authorities for guiding us; they do this not only by words, but also by their shining examples of humility, purity, detachment, selflessness, endurance, forgiveness, compassion and love. Through them we discover that the only "true" religion is the religion of self–realization and universal love.

IV.

The Foundation of the Spiritual Path

Now let us go deeper into the subject itself: How do we find God? How can we realize divine consciousness? How can we approach our Creator? The first condition for finding God is a strong aspiration. Only those who really yearn for God can find Him. God is not an object that can be obtained by will or mind; we have to search for Him with our dedicated hearts. It might be out of pure longing that burns in our soul like an inextinguishable fire, or out of pain or a deep inner loneliness that we might begin to search for the transcendental. These sensations draw or pull us towards Him. King David was praying in his Psalms: "From the depth of my soul I am calling unto Thee," "As the deer yearns for fresh water, so my soul yearns, oh Lord, for Thee," "Pity me, my Lord, I have no strength, heal me, my bones are in torment, my soul is in utter torment. My Lord, how long will You tarry?" Further, "Come back, oh Lord, rescue my soul," and "I am worn out with groaning every night. I drench my pillow and soak my bed with tears." (Ps. 6) Many people perhaps sit down for some minutes, repeat a prayer that they have learned at school or that they read out of a book, many even stay for hours reciting holy hymns, psalms or prayers, but who has such a deep yearning in his heart like King David that he sheds tears in his desperate calling for God? Who really searches for God with his very life and with the essence of his soul?

The *Upanishads* say, "If a man is searching for God like a drowning person is gasping for air, then God will manifest and reveal Himself to His devotee within the twinkling of an eye." A heart kindled with the flame of desperate yearning, devotion or love is like a strong magnet powerfully attracting the grace of God upon himself and mankind. Sri Ramakrishna, a great master and saint of nineteenth century India, used to say, "God is like a loving mother caring for you as if you were her only child. As long as you are satisfied with playing with the toys of this sensual world, struggling for worldly fame or success or pleasures of the senses, she carries on with her duties in running and ruling this universe. But as soon as you drop all of your toys, turning and running towards her with the wholeness of your heart, she will forget all of her duties and run towards you, pull you up to her heart and dry the tears of your eyes and comfort your soul with her tender love and compassion." And Swami Yogananda said, "I was crying like a naughty baby to my Divine Mother until she revealed to me the shining face of infinite light and boundless love." If we really pray from the bottom of our heart God will respond. When He answered the heart-rendering calls of King David, the king would then sing a new song of joy: "My Lord has heard the sound of my weeping, He has heard my petition" (Ps. 6), "Now I rejoice and exult in You, I sing praise to Thy Name" (Ps. 9), "In God alone there is rest for my soul, from Him comes my safety" (Ps. 62), "I take shelter in YHWH. He is the horn of my salvation" (Ps. 18), and "YHWH is the fortress of my life, of whom should I be afraid?" (Ps. 27).

Whether there is longing or pain, loneliness or joy, always be aware that there is nothing in this world that can satisfy the yearning of your soul and nothing that can heal the wounds of your heart except God! He in His infinity is our blessing, our wealth, our remedy. He Himself is the satisfaction of all our desires, the fulfillment of our dreams. He is our joy and our life, our spouse and our friend, our lover and our beloved. He is our All in All.

Of course there are many people who think they lack nothing and that they are happy; they are not aware of their inner emptiness and they have no access to their true selves or even to their feelings. They dissipate themselves in sense pleasures, outer activities and other distractions. Only if we retire from all these distractions might we become aware of where we truly are with ourselves in terms of heart and soul. Often we will find that we are separated not only from God, but also from the depth of our hearts and the awareness of our souls. Without self-awareness, without access to our own heart and feelings we cannot find God. He Who is like a lightning flash, a silent thunder or a mighty and wise king, all in all an ocean of consciousness and bliss, can only be approached and reached with a correct attitude and from the place of our heart.

So we find two other conditions necessary for the search of God: self-awareness and devotion. Without being aware of where we are, and from that getting in touch with our heart and soul, there is "nobody" that can reach out in search for Him. Only a soul can search for

God; mind and a body cannot find Him. We have to go into ourselves, layer by layer, in order to discover ourselves and to reach and free our feeling and loving heart; from that place, where we find ourselves, we reach out for God in conscious awareness and devotion, directing and offering Him the feelings of our heart, our longing, our loneliness, our joy or whatever we find there within ourselves. We offer all that we are to the holy feet of the Lord. Such is the indispensable precondition for our spiritual search and this process of personal reaching out for God is the root of all true prayer and meditation. Without intense prayer and meditation which lead to silent communion with God, we cannot achieve anything on the spiritual path. Every form of prayer and meditation starts from the point where we sit down in silence, withdraw our awareness from the world, the senses and the body and direct it inwardly to search for our self and to get in touch with our heart and feelings. This, in fact, is the crucial point of our search: to find ourselves in the most subtle of our longings and feelings. From there we reach out for God.

Knowing and understanding this simple truth, we can start with our first steps towards a spiritual path. What will happen and what will be our experience on this passageway? There are mainly two kinds of patterns that we can find in the first approaches of the seeker who is beginning his path. The first is that he might rather quickly discover that he does not easily find access to his heart or his feelings. Sitting down, in order to go within and to meditate, he might experience himself like a block of wood or stone, caught in thoughts or dullness, neither being able to shake off nor to offer them to the feet of the Lord in a directed prayer. Or he might reach a state of quietness which he can hold for awhile, but he will fail to dive more deeply to experience the melting of his heart in search for closeness with God and to enter the gates of His all-transforming presence. This kind of experience of dryness, feelinglessness, dullness, lack of concentration, finding oneself caught in thoughts or standing before an unscaleable wall is the most common for the beginner.

The second pattern is the other new seeker who might rather quickly find access to an experience of light or even a tremendous relief or comfort or melting away in intense personal prayers, feeling the soft touch of God's grace opening the floodgates to many tears and feelings. He might be overwhelmed or a least feel deeply thankful for what he has received and through this experience make some immediate changes in his habits or attitudes towards daily life. But after a while he will find himself losing this kind of immediate or easy access to his heart and feelings and to God's grace-bestowing light. Thereupon, he might either slowly become aware that he is approaching a rather different layer of his self which is less comfortable and less easy to penetrate, or he might fall into the delusion that he has now reached what there is to be reached and lull himself into an illusion of imagination that tells him he has now found God. In both cases, the seeker is now reaching a similar inner state or condition of frozenness as mentioned above, the first one moving towards becoming aware of it, the second one being caught in an illusion through lack of awareness.

If, however, one becomes aware of where one is, one

has to continue from that very place. Such a person now has to cope with the same obstacles, the same kind of dryness or hardness of his heart as the other. Here the real work begins. Many people seeking a spiritual path have the expectation that soon everything will be light and easy. But that is not so. As I said before, we might experience some light or joy or peace or comfort in our soul in the beginning, but after a little while we will face one or another kind of wall which separates us from the depth of our heart and from God. In meeting these obstacles which separate us from the Self and God and others, we encounter the first and most essential task of our inner striving and spiritual quest: to tear down the insurmountable wall of spiritual separation from God. This is the most important task of our life and therein lies even the cause and reason for our birth into this world. He who fails in this task, thus failing to get closer and closer to his Lord and Redeemer, is wasting his life. There is nothing more important for us and our soul than to realize God, Who is the true essence of our very life, our existence and the substance of our being. Everything else can wait. If we have attained Him, we have attained everything; if we fail Him, we have failed everything. All other attainments will prove to be as nothing. And in order to find and realize God, we only need to remove the obstacles that separate us from Him.

Having removed the causes of separation, realization is at hand: our soul will merge into this timeless infinity and experience the peace and bliss of Holy Communion, even inseparable Oneness with Him. In other words, in order to realize God, Who is the one true being of all that is, there is nothing to be attained! We only have to remove something – the obstacles that separate us from Him as our true Self. It is as if we would be holding our hand in front of our eyes, not knowing what we miss and what we do. Removing our hand, we see the bright light of the sun and enjoy being warmed by its life–spending rays.

Now the question arises: What are the obstacles that create such a strong wall or deep gulf between God and ourselves? Searching for an answer to this question, we again will find the masters of all ages and traditions in accord with each other. They all agree that it is the ego, with its different faces and facets, that is the root and cause of all separation, emptiness and suffering. If we remove the ego structure, we will see nothing but God. To give some examples, I will refer first to the writings of Isaiah who states: "It is your iniquities that have created a gulf between you and your God. Your sins have made Him veil His face." (Isaiah 59.2) The German mystic Johannes Tauler declares: "Every thread of a thought to be thought outside of God is separating us from Him, but nothing can separate us from Him so deeply as the (individual) soul remaining under the tyranny of its own will." In the first two sentences of Swami Shivananda's book, *The Mysteries of the Mind and Its Control*, he declares: "That which separates you from God is mind. The wall that stands between you and God is (the outward-directed or oriented) mind. If you pull the wall down through devotion you will come face to face with God." And the *Upanishads* of old tell us: "It is only selfishness that keeps us in bondage."

Here we have four statements which seem to differ slightly. While Isaiah is calling the cause of separation "iniquity" and "sin," Johannes Tauler is naming it "thoughts" or "the selfish will." But what else could the root of "iniquity" and "sin" be, other than our "selfish will?" And the root of the selfish will is the ego which is the sum total of all the tendencies rooted in our soul and drawing us from God or separating us from Him. Many masters refer to this cause of separation as our mind. Mind is neither pure consciousness nor cosmic intelligence; it is a bundle of thoughts restlessly arising from the seed of our wrong identification with self and body. And this wrong identification, which is the seed of all our thoughts and selfish tendencies, is the very seed and core of our ego. Actually, we can call the mind the subtle body or operational instrument of the ego. All that we place above God in priority, all that we give more importance to than to God, whether it is a thing, an accomplishment, a person, a tiny thought which keeps our mind busy or all that we cling to, all of these separate us from Him. In fact, it is not the things themselves that separate us from our Source, but the tendencies of our mind which cling to them that are the obstacles causing the division.

Ego, wrong identification, iniquity, selfishness, selfish will, attachment, a clinging mind or sin are only different names for the same thing. Sin is nothing other than that which creates separation and its very cause is the ego, which is the cause of all suffering. If there were no ego, there would be no one to cling or to create any separation and no one to suffer from it. Ego manifests in different forms: as selfish thoughts or deeds, pride and arrogance, as carelessness, hardness of heart, feelinglessness, dullness, emptiness, as desires and emotions, such as anger, jealousy, hatred, revenge and many, many others. Often we have managed to refrain from the outer expression of the gross forms of these tendencies and emotions, but that does not mean that they are not there within us. It only means that we have suppressed or frozen them somewhere in our soul. As soon as we search for God or the depth of our heart, we meet these frozen tendencies and emotions in the form of hardness, feelinglessness or a wall which we run against, not discovering its origin.

Many people think, "I have done nothing extremely wrong in this life, so what can really separate me from God?" But we do not see into the past; most of the tendencies and emotions, the obstacles and walls that separate us from Him have their roots in what we did in our past lives. It is not the little mistakes, but the great wrongs, the misdeeds (sins) of many incarnations that manifest as obstacles and walls in our soul. Nowadays, many people deny the fact of previous incarnations or deny their relevance, but most of the world religions, such as Hinduism, Buddhism and Judaism, explicitly deal with the concept of reincarnation as a natural course of life and the unfoldment of our hidden potentials. In Judaism it is explicitly dealt with in Kabbalah and mysticism; the prophets, for example, take this knowledge for granted as part of a common understanding. Institutional Christianity denies the fact of reincarnation, even though its existence becomes obvious in reading its basic scriptures.

At any rate, the denial of reincarnation is a matter of suppression of the inconvenient truths about our past, lying dormant in our souls. We try to escape responsibility for our past by rejecting the fact of its existence or relevance. We play it down and neglect it and hope to, therefore, shake off all of our responsibility. But the fruits of our past deeds will always be with us. There is a saying that one harvests according to what one sows; if one sows lilies, he will harvest lilies; if one sows thorns, he will reap thorns. The ground into which one sows the seed is our soul and, depending on the seed, it will bear fruit: good or evil, virtue or vice. As God says to Moses, "I set before you a blessing and a curse; a blessing if you obey My command, a curse if you disobey and leave the way that I have marked out for you...." (Deuter. 11.26-28) The harvest of a life is the virtue or the vice, the light or the darkness we have gained within our soul in that lifetime. This truth within will either accuse or defend us before the Face of God. We can not escape this law. Like Adam or Jonah, who tried to escape from their destiny but were caught up by God and His judgment, so too will we be caught up by the aftereffects of our past deeds. They are always following us like a shadow since they are manifest within our own soul. To express it even more clearly: it is the guilt from our past lives, called by the eastern traditions "karma", that is the true obstacle in both our daily life and our spiritual path. Today nobody likes this term "guilt" and many try to explain it away with psychological arguments, but it is exactly what Isaiah is meaning with the terms "iniquities" and "sin." Whenever the prophets accuse the people of Israel or any other nation of failing the path of God, calling them to return to righteousness in order to receive His mercy, they are not so much concerned with their actual ignorance, disobedience and worldliness, but with their roots in the far past, "in the days of old."

Just as ego and karma are two faces of the same thing or two sides of the same coin, "sin", "karma" and "guilt" are synonyms. The original sin that created the first split from God is the root and seed of the ego and the ego is the root of all further iniquities, impurities and failures. There is no other direct way than to cope with this fact and to take responsibility for what we have done and become. As one says, "One becomes what one thinks," or "We have become what we have thought."

There is another group of people that are deluded by another form of self–denial: the vast mass of people that believe that they are and always were "victims" of others. They see "evil" only outside themselves. If one hints about them being closed or bitter, about their lack of compassion, their hardness of heart or their judgmentalism, they quickly respond: "If you only knew what I have suffered, then you would understand." But they miss the truth! Suffering does not close or harden our hearts; there have been many great souls and faithful devotees of God who have really suffered very much, who were betrayed or disowned by their "friends," humiliated in the presence of their false accusers or even tortured unto death. But they bore all and everything in the name of God without hardening their hearts! Those faithful who survived their tortures are neither bitter nor do they accuse anyone or hate their accusers or tormentors. Since they live a life in God, they experience that God heals all of their wounds and they find forgiveness for everyone.

Worldly people or persons with a strong ego, who neither can bow nor surrender, accuse or blame God for their suffering, even if it is only a material loss or sickness. Such people always say, "Where is God if He lets this happen?" Of course He is right there, but they have not been in Him. By speaking so, they prove that they have never found a personal relationship or closeness to Him. For a man of real faith and devotion, suffering will never bring about a separation from his Beloved, nor a hardening of his heart. In fact, his reaction is the opposite: he experiences every pain that he feels or receives from God as causing an even wider opening of his heart. Such a person understands Buddha's statement, "Whenever the hate of the world is piercing the heart of the Buddha, it will release the flow of his mercy and compassion." You might now think or say, "I am not a Buddha," but the law is the same: whoever is in God will never accuse anyone nor execute revenge for he experiences God's healing mercy and care and a steady growth in forgiveness, love and compassion. Suffering is always an opportunity for growth and a help for softening the heart.

Only ignorant people see the cause of their hardened hearts and their bitterness outside of themselves. In fact, it is not suffering that hardens our heart, but ignorance, selfishness and pride. Nowadays many people are engaged in "New Age Movements." They have heard about karma and reincarnation and through their imagination some even brag about having been some rather glorious kings or queens. But do they investigate what they did in these roles or how cruel, selfish or proud they were in them, if in fact these imaginations would be based on true insights coming from God? If we are truthful with God and ourselves, we have to confess: it is not what we have suffered that separated us from God or hardened our hearts, but it is what we have done or how we have reacted that has caused our suffering now. And we are called upon to take responsibility for it. In Gita Mallasz' book *Talking With Angels,* we find a discourse between master and disciple which refers to this fact: "Question: How could I tear down the wall that is between me and others? Response: The wall is in you. You have built it with your own hands and hid behind it from the Divine." (Discourse from October 8, 1943) Walls are not built to defend our soul, which is invulnerable, but to defend our ego!

So if we think that we have not committed any sins and that our egos are shattered in acts of perfect surrender, then we should reflect how far we are from seeing God or merging into His infinite light and unlimited love and compassion. The first fruits of closeness to God are a soft heart with understanding compassion and a growing detachment from self and world, along with an increasing dispassion and a deepening inner peace and contentment. If we contemplate these basic truths, we will become aware that the search for God is not just an easy walk on the "sunny side of the street" but demands true commitment and perseverance in the task of self-discovery and surrender. We have to be ready to accept and cope with the inconvenient fact that we will not only find a shining, blissful core of divinity within ourselves, but also rather filthy layers of impurities and imperfections that hide or cover our true Godly nature. Diving into the depths of our being in order to lift the treasure of divine light and the crown jewel of our higher self, we first cross and pass rather thick layers of egotism and guilt. As Jeremiah and Isaiah have said: "I have planted you as a precious vine ... and clothed you with purity but you have exchanged your glory for shame... and spotted your clothes with filth."

If we start to take responsibility and look at ourselves with an impartial eye, being ready to cope with the unpleasant and to meet with our shadow, allowing them to shatter our false images of self, we will not only rid ourselves of all of them and develop humility and devotion, but we will also receive God's mercy and love, step-by-step restoring ourselves to our original dignity as human beings and children of God. If we open ourselves for the realization of our iniquities without judging ourselves for them and confess them to our Lord and Creator, He will again lift us up from the lowliness into which we have fallen and purify us through His compassion and grace. Inwardly experiencing His radiant light rising on the horizon of our existence and feeling His tender touch in our hearts will melt away all of our bad habits and comfort us in our pain and repentance.

In his Psalms King David sings, "Happy the man whose faults are forgiven, whose sin is blotted out; happy the man whom YHWH accuses of no guilt, whose spirit is incapable of deceit! All the time I kept silent, my bones were wasting away with groans, day in, day out, day and night. Your hand lay heavy on me, my heart grew parched as stubble in summer drought. At last I admitted to You I had sinned; no longer concealing my guilt I said, 'I will go to the Lord and confess my fault.' And You, You have forgiven the wrong I did, have pardoned my sin." (Ps. 32.1-5)

Intense meditation and sincere self-discovery are the two basic conditions for finding God and returning onto

His path. Truthfulness in our self–discovery and allowance of pain and tears of repentance are the two attitudes that will make our efforts a blessing. It is He Himself who will reveal the origin and nature of our impurities and iniquities which separate us from Him. Seeking Him with utter yearning and truthful devotion, He will help us to see ourselves as in a mirror. Looking into the mirror of His light, we cannot but see ourselves. If we accept these uneasy truths and revelations, we will at the same time receive His purifying mercy and His comforting love. Only He, in His majesty, can purify, transform and restore us to our eternal inheritance as children of light. He is the only true savior and redeemer, the Lord of judgment and mercy. What God wants from us in these self-discoveries is two things: first, a change in our attitudes towards Him, our companions and our own selves and a return to a divine life. In Exodus He states, "I want you to be holy, for I, Your Lord, am holy." Secondly, He wants us to discover from where we have fallen and where we have failed, in order to repair our wrongs and find our way back to our original vocation and calling, to our God-given mission here in this world. Finding our vocational mission and following His calling, we are walking the path of God-realization. Vocation rises and develops from closeness to God and closeness to God merges into the path of His calling: "Do not be afraid, for I have redeemed you; I have called you by your name, you are Mine. Should you pass through the sea, I will be with you, or through rivers, they will not swallow you up. Should you walk through fire, you will not be scorched and the flames will not burn you. For I am the Lord, your God, the Holy One, your Savior." (Isaiah 43.1-3)

Receiving, listening to, obeying and following His call is the moving power of the Holy Spirit in our heart, the invisible force that pulls and draws us closer and closer to Him. It is a life lived in consecration and service. Hearing and following His call, we know and feel that I am His and He is mine: "I am the own of my Beloved and my Beloved is mine." (Song of Songs) Only if we have purified ourselves in the waters of self-knowledge and repentance and surrendered our lives to God's will, only if we, through His glorifying help, have succeeded in self-discipline and self-transformation can we say that we are a true disciple of God. Only if we have found light and peace in our own heart can we bring light and peace to others. Only if we have overcome our slavery to the whims of our animal nature and freed ourselves from inner and outer attachments and dependencies can we bring the message of love and salvation to others. That is the path to liberation and God-realization. A slave can not serve God. He does not belong to Him, but to his senses. And a person of bondage can not preach salvation. It is only a living example of inner realization and God's calling that will invest a person's words with authority and power.

A man that has prepared himself for a vocation and for serving the task of his calling is walking in the light and the power of the Lord, His Creator. He is losing himself in God to be found in Him. His life is a heavenly journey and a holy adventure. He is walking from glory to glory and abyss to abyss until he himself ceases to be and merges into Him: "I Am He and He is I," "Tat-twam-asi," "Ana al haqq," "I Am That I Am" - that is the final realization. As it says in the Proverbs, "Would I have known Him, I had become He."

May He bestow His grace upon us, may He give us truthfulness and courage to walk the narrow path of realization. May He safely guide us through the valley of darkness and quench our thirst with the wine from His cup of salvation. Om. Amin. Amen.

V.

Is a Teacher or a Spiritual Guide Needed?

Many people who are looking for a spiritual path start out by themselves. They buy a couple of books, begin with some form of spiritual exercise or meditation and, forming new concepts about themselves and their lives, think to have found their way. But in fact, it is not that easy. The first problem or question is how to apply the spiritual teachings received through books or study groups to our inner reality and our lives. This is not a mere "technical" problem, but rather a problem of self-awareness and access to spiritual realities and powers. Being inexperienced in bridging the gap from where one is to the realm of divine light, and also being blind about the inner condition of self and ego, one can hardly find or grasp a safe and secure starting point within that is beyond self-delusion. Since our ego is a great master in deluding us with tricks and arguments and with covering and hiding inconvenient facts about ourselves, we will easily be trapped in self-created imaginations or fancies and not be able to truly free our hearts and minds from the many subtle veils that separate us from the reality of spiritual life. If we really are wise, we will understand that we are, to a very great extent, blind to ourselves on the basis of a personal perception and awareness.

Secondly, we are confronted with the question of how to reach out for the Divine. How can we find an inner awakening of our spiritual energy by ourselves? How can we ourselves kindle the flame of spiritual awareness? Of course we can try, but will we succeed? And thirdly, how can we bridge the gap, the abyss that is sparating us from God? How can we cross it safely? How did others manage?

These questions are essential. Of course everyone can and should start by himself and one might even succeed for a while, but after some steps one will either find that he is not making any more progress, or even worse, is unconsciouly caught in some form of self-delusion which keeps him stagnant and far away from the goal he went off to seek and reach. Then we have to ask, what does a person do if he wants to learn some kind of craft or art or science? We all will agree, he will start by looking for a good school or teacher. If one wants to learn the violin, one does not just start scratching around on a fiddle, but looks around for a good musician who really has mastered the art of his instrument. And if one is clever, one will not go to a second-class artist who is just a technician without the reverberation of his soul, but he will go to someone whose heart and soul is resounding with music and who also has the gift of passing on his art to those who sincerely seek to study it. Everyone knows that it is better to start under correct guidance from the beginning than to correct learned mistakes or wrongs later. Also, if one considers climbing a high mountain or crossing a far–off ocean, one will seek an experienced guide who will safely lead him to his destination. In the same way, we have to understand that meditation, self-discovery and the whole path to self-realization is also a very high and subtle art and a long journey across different unknown lands of the soul, mind and spirit and needs careful and experienced guidance. Guidance helps us to reach our goal. In the *Bhagavad Gita* Lord Krishna says to Arjuna, "Many have gone out to seek Me, but of the millions who sought, only one succeeded to really know Me."

Rejecting the idea of having a humble and experienced teacher who has the God-given gift or power of kindling the flame of true aspiration in your heart and of awakening the power of spiritual awareness in your soul and who will lovingly instruct and guide you along the path, is a result of pride, arrogance or distrust. Such a teacher is like a philosopher's stone, able to transform the seeker by his mere touch or look or presence. Of course there are many false teachers, but this is not a reason to reject the idea of the necessity of having a teacher or guide. One needs discrimination and understanding before choosing or accepting someone as a true spiritual guide or messenger of God. Some people even doubt that such a God-guided teacher can be found today in our world, but this is not so. Whenever there is a true thirst for knowledge, light and God-realization, a true guide can be found. Such a guide is not a person of mere book learning or theological study, but one of real self-mastery, absolute pure ethical conduct of life, spiritual enlightenment and God-realization. He has the gift to awaken the spiritual energy in deserving students or devotees, the clear inner vision to point out and correct impurities and misconceptions, weaknesses and blind spots in our little "self" and to slowly guide us though the vast land of our unconscious to the shores of super-consciousness, spiritual realization and eternal life. Such a teacher is called a spiritual preceptor for he has the power to work a total spiritual transformation for the seeking soul. Of course such a teacher is very rare, but nevertheless is accessable to anyone who is sincerely and wholeheartedly striving for self-knowlege and spiritual truth.

The sacred book *Viveka Chudamani* states in its introduction that there are three things which are rare to be obtained. These are:

1. "a worthy human birth,
2. true aspiration for liberation, and
3. a God-realized master helping you to realize this ultimate goal yourself."

A burning thirst for liberation is very rare to be found, but a realized master is even more rare and hard to be found and one requires God's grace to approach such a master. Nevertheless, the divine law grants him whose aspiration is pure to find or meet his guide and teacher, who will, through the course of time, become his dearest friend, loving servant and wise teacher.

To find such a teacher one needs true aspiration and clear discrimination. Meeting a "supposed" spiritual guide, one has first to approach him with an open heart but also with impartial discrimination. If that person is abiding in the high ideals and virtues he is teaching, has the gift of awakening spiritual light in your soul, is without self-interest and selflessly and lovingly engaged in bringing to you understanding, love and inner progress, then you can trust him to be sincere. It still might take some time to really recognize his inner state or whether he is, in fact, your preceptor, but the time will surely come when you will know.

The fact is that we can meet different spiritual people who are able to inspire us, but there is only one teacher who is meant to guide each of us to our final destination and this one is our guide and preceptor. And just as one can not have five violin teachers at one time because each one has a different style and approach, one also can not have several spiritual guides at the same time. God has provided exactly one spiritual preceptor for each one of us and when the time is ripe he will be revealed to us. Until then it is good to follow him whom you have found to be pure in heart, truthful in his words and deeds and capable of kindling your inner light and giving you guidance on the path of meditation and self-discovery. You can follow him with undivided trust because he is always working on a base of immediate guidance by God. In his instructions and his teachings he does not only expound on systems or scriptures, but draws his inspiration directly from universal consciousness and in accordance to the actual needs and psychological factors of the disciples he is presently guiding or instructing. He is in touch with God and his disciples at the same time. So he is acting, guiding and teaching according to the influence and influx of Divine Providence and, in this way, deals even with the unspoken questions and the most hidden concerns of your heart. He helps you to discover and bring forth the precious gifts and treasures of your soul, as well as to become aware of the obstacles that have to be removed. You might even experience such a person as a perfect mirror reflecting both your inborn divinity as well as the dark side of your lower nature.

It does not matter to which creed or religion, which nationality or folk he is belonging to; what does matter is if he has vision of God. If he has this vision, he will somehow subtly radiate His light, love and wisdom and certainly will guide you with a sense of great respect and affection. If you have found such a person, trust him, digest his teaching and follow his instructions. He will open your inner eyes for the invisible and for the great miracles of life. He will guide and protect you and be your closest companion in your quest for truth and enlightenment, even if he himself remains detached. But, he will also be the greatest enemy of your ego! He will make it visible and not allow it to remain hidden or ignored; therefore, the teacher's guidance sometimes is very uncomfortable or even painful (for the ego). He will not allow you to stay in delusion because he has come to impart you with the light and the taste of true Self. If you discover this to be a fact, then you know you have found your true teacher and preceptor of spiritual realization. There is an Indian proverb that says, "It is easier to find a true spiritual guide or teacher than to find a sincere disciple or seeker." In fact, once a journalist from England asked a Tibetan lama why there are so few realized spiritual teachers to be found in the West and the Lama's response was, "Because there are no disciples. Everybody wants to be a teacher! And many, if they have read a couple of books, appoint themselves to be teachers instead of humbling themselves at the feet of a true master who is appointed by God."

To become a disciple of truth and eternal life one must have sincere and unfaltering aspiration. First, one must have a deep yearning for God, for truth or for liberation and second, the willingness to deal with the unpleasant or negative side of one's own self. Thirdly, the willingness to accept and follow the instructions of a true master, even if they are not always to be enjoyed by our egos, must be present. Without these three minimal conditions there is no real progress on the path to God. On the other hand, if you really yearn for God and God-realization and also fulfill the other two conditions, you will certainly find the master of your soul. This is granted by Divine Providence because this is one of God's eternal laws: "Where there is a sincere seeker ready to receive spiritual guidance, the teacher is provided." If you have found such a person follow his instruction sincerely.

There are usually three initial stages of guidance with a teacher. After having met the teacher, we first listen to his teaching, his explanation of the path and the methods he is offering. This time of general instruction is also the time of meeting and getting to know each other; it is also the time to test the teacher and our own readiness to follow his instruction. Usually, if the teacher is competent, this is an easy and beautiful time of good encounters and first steps forward. During the course of these steps we slowly proceed on our path by keeping up our spiritual exercises, awareness and routines in our daily life. After deepening our experience, one day there will arise the feeling for the necessity of a clear commitment in order to advance on the path. At this point one has to pray intensely and to decide whether one wants to really commit his life to the path that is offered by the guide and his group. If one is still not clear by then whether this teacher is his perceptor, his God-given gate for realizing the goal of life, then he will have to clarify this question within himself then and there. One has to be very honest with oneself in this testing and decision because if one does not find himself willing or ready for such a commitment, he will have to leave the presence of the teacher and his group. It is necessary to understand that there is no way of attaining anything that is valuable in life without commitment. And from a certain point onward, a teacher can only guide and reveal to us the tasks and gifts of spiritual realization if we are willing to follow his instruction and his advice. This point of our path corresponds with the closing of the waves behind the Israelites after their passing the Red Sea. From that moment on, they know themselves to be on their way to the Promised Land. In the same way, the one who has found his master and made the commitment to his teaching has also found the true road of his life and the harbor for his soul. He will find himself in peace and in the joyful awareness of where to direct the intentions, energies and actions of his life. He has then found his task and vocation of life and he will feel with a clarity beyond any doubt that in his path he has found the source for the true and lasting satisfaction of his heart and soul. He has then truly embarked his chariot on the highway of God.

VI.

Where Are You Going?

We all are not born into this world to merely struggle for survival or success or for killing our time in temporary enjoyments or sense pleasures, but for a divine purpose and spiritual task. We are not only "dust returning to dust," but spiritual beings provided with heavenly gifts for attaining mastery of life, spiritual liberation and God-conciousness rather than remaining slaves to our animal whims and desires or blinded victims of pride and illusory self-images. Physically we are mammals, but through our spirit we can become angels, seraphs or even gods. Through inner effort and awakening we can be born to a much higher reality and awareness.

The destiny of our lives lies in our own hands. We ourselves can choose to make whatever we want out of our lives. We can stay lowly as we are, we can strive for name and fame, for cultural, material or even religious success, all of which are temporary and fade away with age and death, or we can strive for everlasting goods within, everlasting treasures of our soul. Using the powers of our hearts and minds, we create our own inner world. We are able to create everything; we can create a hell or a heaven within, or we can exploit or sell our souls in order to achieve temporary importance, influence or power. We can experience the passing pleasures of sense indulgence and passions for the price of inner peace, self-contentment, independence and everlasting joy, or we can attain peace of mind, purity of heart, divine virtues, serenity, tranquillity, uncondtional joy, spiritual enlightenment, fullness of life and immortality, lo all the treasures of heaven. We are the masters of our destiny, the captains on our ships. And as we sow, so shall we reap. Sowing selfishness and pride, we shall reap selfishness and pride; sowing peace and love and truthfulness, we shall reap peace and love and truthfulness, and even more: we shall harvest compassion, wisdom, fulfillment and even wealthy and heavenly treasures.

To live only for a worldly purpose is a waste of our life. Not finding God within this lifetime is a waste of a rare God-given opportunity. He who has no knowledge about the lofty destiny of man is living in a pitiful darkness; but he who has seen the lamp of God, who has at least a vague idea or dim glimpse of the higher goal and destination of human life and refuses to follow its calling, unconsciouly adhering to his spiritual darkness, is a fool. He is wasting his life. Swami Yogananda used to say: "Seek for God first, everything else can wait." Do not postpone what you can do today. What you postpone, you will lose.

In this way the sages and seers of all ages never ceased to lift their trumpets to sound God's call: "Wake and rise. Stand up to your divine birthright as sons and daughters of God and realize your heavenly destiny. Do not waste this life with temporary enjoyments but strive for the highest. Come out of the graves of your passions and old habits, of your lowliness and impurity. Lift the banner of an inspired spiritual life, break the bonds of egotism and selfishness, widen your vision and awareness of life and strive for the beatific shores of enlightenment and liberation."

He who seeks, will find. If one knocks at the gates of heaven, they will be opened. But to put one's foot on the path to self-realization, one needs decisiveness, endurance and courage. It takes a spirit of trust and adventure, the courage to set out for new experiences, the courage to explore new lands and dimensions, the courage to leave old habits and the courage to change and be open for something shining and new, open for an experience of unspeakable truths and intangible realities, but with the security and enjoyment of God's protection and grace and His light shining upon you like the sun upon a newly cultivated garden.

He who has read these lines and has felt the resonance of truth in his heart, the voice of his own conscience and self in these words may reflect about his life, may ponder the thoughts offered to him in this little book and watch the running course of his life in the riverbed of time. How much time do I have? What have I achieved? How much have I discovered and realized of my true inner Self? How much time is left? When will death come? Is that what I have found until now really the ultimate answer to my soul's quest? Who am I? Why have I been created? What is my message to the world? Go and sit somewhere alone, sit in nature and breathe the breath of life, listen to the voice of your heart so you will see if you have set the ship of your life asail for the shores you really want to reach or if you are caught in the backwaters of superficial worldliness and shallow self-contentment. There is always a chance to change but we have to grasp it, otherwise we will only wake up when it is too late.

May God bless you with His quickening Light, may He awaken and expand your self-awareness and give you a clear vision of your eternal inheritance. And may He strengthen and guide you to realize it in this life.

Recommended Reading

On Spirituality:

Paramahansa Yogananda: *Autobiography of a Yogi,* Self-Realization Fellowship, Calif.

Joel Goldsmith: *From Enlightenment to Realization,* De Vorss Publisher, USA

Swami Chidananda: *A Guide to Noble Living,* The Divine Life Society, India; *Path Beyond Sorrow,* The Divine Life Society, India

Mikhael Aivanhov: *Man's Two Natures, Human and Divine,* Prosveta Publ., France; *The Tree of the Knowledge of Good and Evil,* Prosveta Publ., France

Hazrat Inayat Khan: *The Way of Illumination,* Motilal Banarsidass Publ., Delhi

Swami Muktananda: *Where Are You Going?* SYDA Foundation, N.Y.

On Religion and Interreligious Understanding:

Paramahansa Yogananda: *The Science of Religion,* Self-Realization Foundation, Calif.

Anthony Elenjimittam: *Interreligious Understanding,* Aquinas Publ., Bombay

Hazrat Inayat Khan: *The Unity of Religious Ideals,* Motilal Banarsidass Publ., Delhi

General Ideas:

Z'ev Ben Shimon Halevi: *A Kabbalistic Universe,* Rider Publ., London; *The Way of Kabbalah,* Rider Publ., London

Swami Muktananda: *Kundalini – The Secret of Life,* SYDA Foundation, N.Y.

Max Mordechai Teon: *A Way of Meditation in the Light of Kabbalah,* Argamon, Israel

On Karma and Reincarnation:

Mikhael Aivanhov: *Man, Master of His Destiny,* Prosveta Publ., France

Elisabeth Haich: *Initiation,* Unwin Paperbacks, London

On Spiritual Teachers:

Amrit Desai: *Working Miracles of Love,* Kripalu Publ., Lenox, Mass.

Irina Tweedie: *Daughter of Fire,* Blue Dolphin Publ., England